GOOD NEWS
for
BAD TIMES

A Study of 1 Peter

Richard W. De Haan
and
Herbert Vander Lugt

While this book is designed for the reader's personal use and profit, it is also intended for group study. A leader's guide is available from your local bookstore or from the publishe

D1021638

VICTOR BOOKS
a division of SP Publications, Inc.
WHEATON. ILLINOIS 60187

Library of Congress Catalog Card Number: 75-6146
ISBN 0-88207-719-8

© 1975 by SP Publications, Inc. World rights reserved
Printed in the United States of America

VICTOR BOOKS
A division of SP Publications, Inc.
P.O. Box 1825 • Wheaton, Illinois 60187

Contents

Preface

Bad times may come upon even the most devoted Christian. When they do, fellow-believers should manifest genuine compassion, gladly giving of themselves for the well-being of their brothers and sisters in Christ.

But positive actions are not all we can offer. In Peter's first epistle we learn that suffering and sorrowing people need more than anything else to be instructed in the spiritual realities of the Christian faith. They must recognize that they are pilgrims and strangers on their way to their eternal home. They must be reminded in a loving manner that it is far more important to be ready for heaven than to enjoy physical comforts here. They must know that character and conduct, combined with an intelligent witness to the truth, can do more lasting good than the finest program of social welfare and economic relief.

The best news of all for believers is that God is able to use bad times to make us better people, and that He will give us grace to be triumphant in all kinds of trouble.

We pray that this book will be used by the Lord to impress these great truths upon the hearts and minds of all who read it.

We express our appreciation to Clair Hess, director of Radio Bible Class publications, and to David Egner, assistant to the president of Radio Bible Class, for their editorial work. A special word of thanks is also due to Lois Weber and Audree Van Ryn for typing the manuscript.

Richard W. De Haan
Herbert Vander Lugt

1

This Election Can't Be Lost

(1 Peter 1:1-2)

A letter from a loved one, especially if it comes when you're lonely, discouraged, or oppressed, is encouraging and uplifting. When you see the familiar handwriting or recognize the home address, your heart is immediately lifted, and the cheery words of understanding and hope make the burdens light and the pathway easier.

The Christians in Asia Minor were undergoing persecution. For the first time, opposition and hardship had entered their lives. How they had welcomed the message of the Gospel when they heard it from faithful missionaries of Jesus Christ! Happy in the Lord, they delighted in the hope of eternal salvation, and were growing steadily in the faith. They had formed churches and were meeting regularly for prayer, instruction, and fellowship. The first blush of Christian happiness still glowed in their hearts.

But then trouble arose! In Rome, the godless emperor Nero had singled out Christians to be the scapegoats for problems he had brought on himself. Many believers there had been imprisoned, tortured, or put to death for their faith. Procurators and governors throughout the empire were oppressing and harassing the children of God, including these believers in Asia Minor.

The Christians scattered throughout the provinces wondered if God had suddenly decided to withdraw His favor, or if He was punishing them for some sin they hadn't confessed. You see, they didn't have the advantage of the complete New Testament as we do. They couldn't read Jesus' words of warning that they would be hated by the world, nor His promise of gracious provision for their every need.

You can imagine, therefore, the excitement that spread through the churches when the news that Peter, respected and deeply loved disciple of the Lord Jesus, had written them a letter. It was being circulated throughout their provinces, and would soon arrive at their church.

Finally it came! All eyes were upon the leader, and every heart beat faster, as he stood before the congregation, carefully unrolled the scroll, and began to read:

> Peter, an apostle of Jesus Christ, to the sojourners scattered throughout Pontus, Galatia, Cappadocia, Asia, and Bithynia, elect according to the foreknowledge of God, the Father, through sanctification of the Spirit, unto obedience and sprinkling of the blood of Jesus Christ: Grace unto you, and peace, be multiplied (1 Peter 1:1-2).

What a comfort to every believer listening! Peter was assuring them that they had been chosen as the special recipients of God's redeeming grace. He was reminding them that since they were aliens and pilgrims in this world, they had no right to expect life to be a continual "bed of roses." Then he spoke of the "sanctification of the Spirit," telling them they had been set apart as saints.

These words must have been greatly encouraging; in fact, this entire epistle is filled with hope, promise, and help for suffering Christians.

Peter begins his letter by giving three identifying marks of the Christian: he is a *sojourner* in this world, the *elect* of God, and a *saint*. When suffering oppression, one can easily become confused and lose perspective. American prisoners of war, subjected to a rigorous brainwashing effort, were greatly heartened by singing the "Star Spangled Banner" and quoting the pledge of allegiance to the American flag. This helped keep alive their pride in the United States and their hope of returning someday. So, too, as God's children we can keep our identity in clear focus by seeing ourselves, even during great trial, as *sojourners, elect,* and *saints*. In this chapter, therefore, we'll consider each of these in careful detail, though in different order.

Believers Are the Elect

One distinctive of all Christians is that they are the chosen of God. Peter says, "Elect according to the foreknowledge of God, the Father" (1 Peter 1:2). Whenever the term *election* is mentioned, it raises questions in the minds of many people. They wonder how the teaching that God has chosen some for eternal salvation can be reconciled with the biblical emphasis upon man's responsibility and upon his free will.

One reason for the confusion is that people are inclined to take an extreme position. Some theologians might be called hyper-Calvinists. They say that God in eternity past chose some to be saved and at the same time decreed that others should be damned. Such theologians put all the emphasis on God's sovereign choice and deny that man's free will has any part in it. They contend that everyone is either predestined by God to be saved or predestined to be condemned.

Other theologians have taken the opposite view, and for all practical purposes deny God's sovereignty. They say the Lord foreknew who would believe on Jesus, and that He chose them on that basis. According to this view, everything depends upon man's will. This leads to the misconception that an individual can go through life with alternating periods of being saved and lost. Such believers do not possess the blessed assurance of having been chosen by God nor the confidence that He will keep them saved until they receive their inheritance in heaven.

I believe that the truth regarding election and free will can be found somewhere between these two extreme positions. Both election and free will are taught in the Word of God. We must acknowledge that God has indeed chosen some to be saved, but we must also recognize that man has a will and that he is a responsible moral being. Having said that, we must admit that to our finite human comprehension this is a mystery beyond full understanding.

Observe how the fact of God's election is clearly taught in the Scriptures. The Apostle Paul, for example, declared, "According as He [God] hath chosen us in Him [Christ] before the foundation of the world, that we should be holy and without blame before Him, in love having predestinated us unto the adoption of sons by Jesus Christ to Him-

self, according to the good pleasure of His will"
(Eph. 1:4-5; see also Rom. 8:29-30).

Many other passages concerning election might
be adduced, but these references from Paul, added
to Peter's "elect according to the foreknowledge of
God, the Father," should be adequate to represent
the basic truth on this subject. From them we can
draw the following conclusions: (1) God elected
some to be saved. (2) His election was not based
upon any merit He saw in man, but grounded entirely in His good pleasure. (3) This election took
place in eternity past, before the worlds were created. (4) God's election is "according to foreknowledge." This does not mean that God made His
choice simply on the basis of what He knew men
would do, but it does indicate that His election and
His foreknowledge are in perfect harmony.

On the other hand, the Bible complements this
truth by teaching man's individual responsibility to
believe. In fact, the Lord repeatedly invites all men
to be saved. The best-known verse in the Bible declares, "For God so loved the world, that He gave
His only begotten Son, that whosoever believeth in
Him should not perish, but have everlasting life"
(John 3:16).

The Apostle Paul expressed the same universal
offer of redemption by faith, saying, "For whosoever shall call upon the name of the Lord shall be
saved" (Rom. 10:13).

One of the last verses of the Bible issues this
glorious invitation: "And let him that is athirst
come. And whosoever will, let him take the water
of life freely" (Rev. 22:17).

So, there you have it. Both the election of God
and the free will of man are taught in the Scriptures. To top it all off, both ideas are put together

in one sentence. The Lord Jesus said, "All that the Father giveth Me shall come to Me; and him that cometh to Me I will in no wise cast out" (John 6:37). There it is! Election and free will in the same statement. God does His part and we must do ours. He does the electing, but we must receive the salvation He offers by believing on Jesus Christ.

This seems paradoxical to our finite minds. It appears contradictory to accept the fact of sovereign election on the one hand, yet emphasize the reality of man's free will on the other. But both truths are presented in the Scriptures, and we must accept them with the assurance that somehow they harmonize in the infinite counsels of God.

An illustration of a railroad track has often been used and may offer some help. Let's call one rail "election" and the other "free will." The theological train of Bible truth needs both rails. If you remove the rail of man's free will, you crash into the ditch of fatalism. If you remove the rail of sovereign election, you will find yourself in the mire of a works-salvation and fearful insecurity. Both sides of the truth must be accepted and believed. If we gaze down a railroad track to the horizon, we see that in the distance the two rails seem to merge into one. So these two great truths find real harmony in the mind of God.

We who have received Christ can know beyond a shadow of a doubt that we are "elect, according to the foreknowledge of God," as Peter wrote. In the face of adversity, we can take great comfort in saying, "God knew me before the foundation of the world. He singled me out, along with many others, to be one of His own. He destined me to share the full glories of His redemption. I responded, and now the promises of the Bible are mine. I can stand undaunted in Christ, whatever may come my way!"

Pilgrims and Aliens

A second identifying mark of Christians is that they are "sojourners" (1 Peter 1:1, called "strangers" in the King James). This is a good translation of the Greek word *parepidēmois*, for it combines the two ideas, "pilgrim" and "alien," which are inherent in the meaning.

This term accurately describes the relationship of the Christian to this world. Elect of God and redeemed by our faith in Jesus Christ, we have become the citizens of heaven. We are here on earth only temporarily; our face is set toward our heavenly homeland.

The Apostle Paul told the Philippian believers, "For our citizenship is in heaven, from where also we look for the Saviour, the Lord Jesus Christ, who shall change our lowly body, that it may be fashioned like His glorious body, according to the working by which He is able to subdue all things unto Himself" (Phil. 3:20-21).

As the old spiritual says, "This world is not my home; I'm just a-passin' through." The author of Hebrews wrote, "For here have we no continuing city, but we seek one to come" (Heb. 13:14).

As *pilgrims*, we are walking by faith through foreign territory, keeping in mind our heavenly citizenship and eternal home. As *aliens*, we should not be surprised when this world treats us with hostility. In a sense, we don't belong here. We're strangers to its entire value system and view of life. We ought not feel too comfortable, nor settle down to enjoy the best this earth has to offer. In fact, if we begin to feel too much at home here, we

ought to beware, for "our citizenship is in heaven."
We must guard our identity as God's children, lest
it fade away and be corrupted by the qualities of
the foreign land we're crossing.

Also included in the term *sojourner* is the idea of
purpose and goal. We are not vagabonds who just
wander aimlessly. Our sights are set for heaven, and
as we journey, our calling is to do the will of God
and be His ambassadors of redeeming grace.

The believers in the infant church lived in keeping with their "sojourner" status. Barclay, quoting
the famous *Epistle to Diognetus* written by an un-
believing government official, records these historic
words:

> Christians are not marked out from the rest
> of mankind by their country or their speech
> or their customs. . . . They dwell in cities
> both Greek and barbarian, each as his lot is
> cast, following the customs of the region in
> clothing and in food and in the outward things
> of life generally; yet they manifest the won-
> derful and openly paradoxical character of
> their own state. They inhabit the lands of
> their birth, but as temporary residents thereof;
> they take their share of all responsibilities as
> citizens, and endure all disabilities as aliens.
> Every foreign land is their native land, and
> every native land is a foreign land. . . . They
> pass their days upon earth, but their citizen-
> ship is in heaven.*

The early church fathers were keenly aware of
being "sojourners." Tertullian said of the believer,
"He knows that on earth he has a pilgrimage, but
that his destiny is in heaven." Clement of Alexandria

---

* William Barclay, *The Letters of James and Peter,*
(Westminster Press, Philadelphia) pp. 198-199.

declared, "We have no fatherland on earth." Augustine wrote, "We are sojourners exiled from our fatherland."

You can be certain that the persecuted believers to whom Peter was writing found comfort in being called "sojourners." This assured them that their suffering was not to be construed as punishment by God. It reminded them that as Christians they were a distinct people who by their faith in Christ had become aliens in a world where the majority do not believe. It helped them realize that hatred by the ungodly is a natural reaction of the unregenerate to the righteous conduct of people who know the Lord Jesus.

Peter's letter also told the believers that present suffering is only temporary, and that a fadeless, wonderful eternity in heaven is just ahead. It challenged them to be faithful and courageous while traveling through this world. And we today should also see that as aliens and pilgrims we have both a glorious privilege and a solemn responsibility.

Saints

In addition to identifying Christians as *elect* of God and *sojourners,* Peter also referred to them as *saints* —chosen "through sanctification of the Spirit." Since the Greek word translated *sanctification* in this verse has the same root as the term which is always rendered *saints* in the New Testament, and since both have the basic idea of "separation unto God," believers can rightly be called *saints.* We are "set apart" or "sanctified" by the Holy Spirit for the worship and service of God, and belong to the Lord in a unique way.

Sainthood begins at the moment of salvation, and even the most humble believer is a saint. This is illustrated in an article by a missionary in South America. He told about a great new cathedral that had been completed recently, but could not be used for religious festivals because the statues of certain "saints" had not yet arrived from Italy. The missionary then added, "Yet just down the street from that magnificent structure a group of the city's poorest people were meeting in a small storefront mission. In their simple services, saints were being made every day as men and women gave their hearts to Jesus Christ." Yes, everyone who has accepted Him as personal Saviour is a saint.

But sometimes the saints don't act very saintly. The term does not imply that we no longer sin, nor that we have no need to confess our sins and to experience the Lord's forgiveness. In fact, the second of the two statements Peter connects with our being "sanctified through the Spirit" suggests exactly the opposite. First, it is "unto obedience," and second, it is unto "sprinkling of the blood of Jesus Christ." God expects us to obey His will but also to experience the joy of daily cleansing as we walk in fellowship with Him. Let's consider both of these further.

Unto Obedience

The Holy Spirit "sanctifies" us so that we will bring honor and praise to the Lord by a life of obedience. By word and deed we are to "magnify His name." The ideal has been set. We are to follow the example of the Lord Jesus, who said repeatedly that He had come to do His Father's will. He was "obedient unto death, even the death of the cross" (Phil. 2:8).

As the vessels of the tabernacle and temple were to be used only for worship and service of Jehovah, we too are "set apart" to the working of His will.

This means that as Christians our lives are to be in keeping with the principles revealed in God's Word. Our homes should reflect His presence. Our churches should be characterized by humility, co-operation, and love. We should obey the laws of our community, and set a good example. Why? Because ultimately, in all these areas, we are rendering obedience unto the Lord.

Unto Sprinkling

But the fact remains, we're still going to sin. Not a day goes by that is not marred by some evil deed or thought. The Lord, in His marvelous grace and by His sacrifice on the cross, has provided for us the means of daily cleansing. Peter was speaking of this when he said we are sanctified "unto sprinkling of the blood of Jesus Christ."

The basis for his statement is found in the Old Testament ceremonial system. In certain of the rituals, the blood of the sacrificial animals was sprinkled in specified areas. This sprinkling had three different meanings.

First, it signified cleansing. The person who had been cured of leprosy, for example, went before the priest, and blood was sprinkled to indicate that he was now free from the disease and "clean" (Lev. 14: 1-7).

Second, this act was used to symbolize the ratification of a covenant between God and man. Whenever Jehovah and His people entered into a covenant, it was sealed by the sprinkling of the blood of a sacrificial animal (see Ex. 24:3-8).

Third, the application of blood designated certain articles of the tabernacle or temple as set apart for worship. From that point on, the vessel was used exclusively for the service of the Lord (see Ex. 29: 20-22).

The "sprinkling" of 1 Peter 1:2 refers to *cleansing* from sin. Though we have been set apart "unto obedience," we falter and fail every day. Therefore we need daily cleansing, and this is symbolized by the sprinkling of blood. The Apostle John emphasized this truth when he wrote to believers, "If we confess our sins, He is faithful and just to forgive us our sins, and to cleanse us from all unrighteousness" (1 John 1:9). Whenever we are conscious that we have sinned, we must confess it to the Lord. As we do, the sprinkled blood is applied to our souls, and we can go forward in the joy that our fellowship with the Lord has been restored.

Daily cleansing is a blessed privilege, and keeps the relationship between the believer and God at the sweetest and highest level. Sin disrupts the Christian's fellowship with God. It's not our salvation that is put in jeopardy when we sin, but our communion with the Lord. Perhaps an illustration will help.

I'm a son of Dr. M. R. De Haan, and I always will be. When as a boy I was disobedient and broke the commands of my father, the relationship between us would become strained. Our fellowship as father and son was hindered, and was not restored until things were made right. But I remained a De Haan. Nothing could alter that.

So too with Christians. By our faith in the Saviour we are "sons of God, and joint-heirs with Christ." This will never be changed. But sin breaks our fellowship with the heavenly Father, and brings loss of joy and peace. That's why the Holy Spirit's sanctifying work "unto sprinkling of the blood of Jesus Christ" is so important, and I would urge you to come before the Lord daily in confession, and to enjoy the blessing of unbroken communion with God.

Summary

Every Christian is a greatly privileged person. Think of it! You were in God's plan from all eternity. Though millions upon millions of people have lived and died on our planet and we individually are so insignificant that few would notice our departure, God knew us before He created the world. He chose us and destined us to spend eternity with Him in heaven. We may have few talents. We may be lonely. We may be in poor health. We may sometimes get discouraged. But we must never allow ourselves to be plunged into despair. You and I as individuals are important to God. Each of us has a special place in His program, both in this world and in the one toward which we are traveling.

We can also give thanks because we are sojourners. What a difference it makes when we realize that we are not part and parcel of this wicked world! Instead, we are rapidly moving through it to our eternal home. Robert Louis Stevenson said that an old muck farmer was asked if he never got tired of working in the wet soil, and he answered, "He that has something ayont [beyond] need never weary." Thank God, we have something beyond!

Finally, we have the glorious honor of being "sanctified through the Spirit." Each child of God is a saint, set apart by the Spirit for the Lord. He has called us to obedience, but also has made gracious provision for all of our failures. He who chose us to eternal glory applies the blood of Christ to us every time we confess our sins, and He will do so until we reach our destination. What assurance!

If you have never received Jesus Christ, don't make the mistake of becoming fatalistic just because the Bible speaks of election. Someone may say, "If I'm elected, I will come; and if not, it wouldn't do any good for me to try." But that's not what the Bible teaches. It extends an invitation to you and tells you that you must respond in faith. Jesus said, "Come unto Me, *all* ye that labor and are heavy laden, and I will give you rest" (Matt. 11:28). The offer is to everyone—including you! But you must believe. And when you do, you will receive the joyous assurance that you have been chosen from all eternity to be God's child. You will enter into all the spiritual riches indicated by the words, *elect, sojourners,* and *saints.*

2

You Can Faith the Future

(1 Peter 1:3-16)

Salvation is the greatest of all blessings. It beats money, friends, and health. Nothing this world has to offer can even compare to it. It gives us the most wonderful of all benefits—the happiness of being at peace with God and a confidence regarding eternity.

The glory of our great salvation was evidenced to many viewers of the "Mike Douglas Show" some time ago. A young woman totally paralyzed, who does oil paintings by holding the brushes in her teeth, asserted her faith in God's promises. She witnessed boldly of her salvation, and stressed her belief that "all things work together for good to them that love God" (Rom. 8:28). She said she knew her affliction was God's way of conforming her to the image of Jesus Christ (see Rom. 8:29). All the money in the world can't buy a joyous attitude like this. Neither can friends, even if they are many and influential. It comes only through salvation!

Our belief in Christ is not a "fair-weather faith." Nor is it a "for nice people only" salvation. It provides for *every* human need. It delivers from the

19

slavery of drink. It releases from the bondage of lust. It gives victory over greed, hate, fear, bitterness, and despair. It brings joy in the face of suffering. Yes, believers have every right to rejoice in their great salvation!

The Christians who received Peter's first letter were facing persecution. They had become bewildered and discouraged, and they needed help. The apostle wrote to tell them that the riches of their salvation could give them joy and victory even in these circumstances. His opening words of greeting, therefore, were followed by a burst of praise. We can imagine Peter saying, "I know you're going through a difficult time, and I am going to give you some help and encouragement. But first, let's just praise the Lord for His great salvation. Join me in a doxology!"

Blessed be the God and Father of our Lord Jesus Christ . . . (1 Peter 1:3).

Peter then proceeded to name and describe some of the glories of our great salvation. These early Christians, beset with troubles, had not yet learned that their blessings far outweighed their distresses. They were sighing when they should have been singing!

Peter declared four great facts about our salvation, and challenged every believer to a life of gratitude to God. As we look at these truths in detail, I trust that you will become more keenly aware of the wonder of *your* salvation, and that you will resolve to bring honor and glory to the Lord Jesus Christ in every circumstance of your life.

It Gives a Living Hope
The first wonderful fact about the Christian's salvation is the hope it generates within his heart.

Peter says that God has "begotten us again unto a living hope by the resurrection of Jesus Christ from the dead, to an inheritance incorruptible, and undefiled, and that fadeth not away, reserved in heaven for you" (1 Peter 1:3-4).

The Christian's hope is not mere wishful thinking. It's far more than just a vague feeling that everything will turn out all right in the end. His hope is really "faith looking forward," and is based upon God's works and words. This "living hope" begins with the new birth, is certified by the empty tomb, and eagerly anticipates a new home depicted in the Scriptures.

It Begins with a Miracle

One way we know the Christian hope is real is that it has been placed in our hearts by a miracle. Peter tells us that God has "begotten us again unto a living hope." The words *begotten again* bring to mind Christ's statement to Nicodemus, "Ye must be born again" (John 3:7). The New Testament teaches us that at the very instant a person believes on Christ, he receives a new life. He becomes a "new creation" (2 Cor. 5:17). This birth from above is an absolute necessity for entrance into heaven because everyone by nature is "dead in trespasses and sins" (Eph. 2:1), and spiritually blind (1 Cor. 2:14). Nothing short of the miracle of regeneration can give life to those who are dead in sin, or spiritual sight to those who are utterly blind to God and His Word.

The new birth brings with it a new perception of life and reality. It brings an awareness of truths never known before. Through the ministry of the Holy Spirit, the believer is not only given new life, he is *enlightened*. The result is a "living hope" that can never be extinguished.

It Rests on a Solid Basis

We also know our hope is real because it is built upon a solid, logical basis—the resurrection of Christ. The Old Testament saints looked forward to resurrection, but they could believe in it only because of their confidence in what God had said. This is good reason for belief, of course, but today we have the record of the actual historical event. Some of the very men who saw Christ after He arose were the writers of the New Testament Scriptures, and their books come to us with unassailable authenticity. Yes, the resurrection of Jesus Christ is a proven fact of history, and gives us the foundation for believing that we too will go to heaven.

Christ's victory over the grave is our guarantee of resurrection, and of eternal life in heaven. This is the point of Paul's declaration that Jesus was "raised again for our justification" (Rom. 4:25). Our Saviour was delivered to death because of our sins (for He was sinless), and was brought out of the grave by the power of God "because of" our justification. That is, by resurrecting Jesus, God declared that He was satisfied with Christ's payment for our sins. The penalty for our iniquities has been paid in full and therefore the power of death, which is the penalty for sin, has been effectively destroyed.

That's why you and I can base our hope upon our Lord's resurrection. It tells us that our sins have been paid for, and that death cannot hold us in its grip.

It Imparts the Prospect of Glory

Our Christian hope becomes even more precious because of the everlasting glory that awaits us. Peter says that it is an "inheritance incorruptible, and undefiled, and that fadeth not away" (1 Peter 1:4). To understand the full meaning of the verse, let us consider the three expressions which describe our inheritance.

First, the new home that awaits us is "incorruptible." The Greek word Peter used had the meaning of "unspoilable" in his day, denoting a territory considered so secure that no invading force could destroy it. Every Jewish believer was sadly aware that the land of Palestine had been overrun by enemies time after time, and the Gentile believers knew that the mighty armies of Rome had trodden down that entire area of the world. Peter assures believers that their heavenly inheritance is perfectly safe and indestructible.

Then, too, the believer's heritage is "undefiled." Not a country in the world is free from sexual immorality, selfish greed, and cruel criminality. Ungodly, blasphemous religious systems continue to flourish. But in the home that awaits believers, sinners will not come with their evil practices. No gambling halls, no X-rated movie houses, and no pornographic literature will ever be found there. We'll be delivered from every sin, and we'll see no reminder of its effects. The Apostle John portrayed this aspect of the New Jerusalem when he wrote, "And there shall in no way enter into it anything that defileth, neither he that worketh abomination, or maketh a lie" (Rev. 21:27).

The gloryland is also permanent and unchanging: "and that fadeth not away" are Peter's words. How unlike this world! The beauty of Solomon's temple lasted only a short time. The magnificence of great cities like Babylon and Rome gradually disappeared. The loveliness of flowers fades all too quickly. And man himself is described in the Bible as being like the grass of the field that withers under the summer sun. Or like the ocean foam that vanishes as quickly as it comes. But in heaven nothing will ever be dulled, dimmed, or destroyed. As the ages of eternity roll, neither our surroundings nor our persons will diminish in beauty.

Yes, our great salvation gives us a real and lasting hope. It is unrivaled by anything the world can offer, for it has been divinely implanted through the new birth, it is grounded upon the resurrection of Jesus Christ, and it looks forward to an eternal inheritance glorious beyond description!

It Affords a Joyous Certainty

The second wonderful fact about our great salvation is the absolute assurance that we will one day obtain all that God has promised us. Peter says that this "inheritance incorruptible, and undefiled, and that fadeth not away," is "reserved in heaven for you, who are kept by the power of God through faith unto salvation ready to be revealed in the last time" (1 Peter 1:4-5).

The central thought here is that we are kept by God's power through faith. What a comforting thought! We live in an environment that is hostile to our spiritual development. We can neither save nor keep ourselves. But, thank God, He does it for us! The Greek word for *kept* means "to build a fortress around." Within God's garrison we are beyond all danger.

We have this security "through faith." God makes sure we will keep on believing. Peter knew this truth through personal experience.

Remember the events of the night before Jesus' death? Peter had boasted he would never forsake or deny the Lord. The Saviour had rebuked him, telling him that before morning he would deny his Master three times. And that's exactly what happened! Immediately after the third denial, the Lord Jesus looked at Peter with love-filled eyes, and the grieving apostle went out and wept bitterly.

From John 21 we learn that the resurrected Saviour lovingly forgave and restored Peter. All through those three denials the outspoken disciple never stopped being a child of God. He never really lost his faith. Why? Because God had "built a fortress" about Peter in answer to prayer, for Jesus had said, "Simon, Simon, behold, Satan hath desired to have you, that he may sift you as wheat; but I have prayed for thee, *that thy faith fail not*" (Luke 22: 31-32).

Now, as Peter wrote his letter, he was keenly aware that God had kept him "through faith." That's why he could honestly promise these persecuted first-century believers that God would see them safely home to glory. How wonderful the assurance of our eternal redemption!

It Gives Meaning to Life's Trials

Third, our great salvation explains the meaning of our suffering and trials. We are assured that we will profit from them, both in this world and the next. "In this ye greatly rejoice, though now for a season, if need be, ye are in heaviness through manifold trials, that the trial of your faith, being much more precious than of gold that perisheth, though it be tried with fire, might be found unto praise and honor and glory at the appearing of Jesus Christ" (1 Peter 1:6-7).

"More precious than gold"? Yes, that's what Peter said. Earthly riches last only for a little while. But what we suffer for Christ will bring eternal praise, honor, and glory at His coming.

We must not become bitter, therefore, nor wallow in self-pity when suffering comes. We are to view it as the overture to a grand, heavenly oratorio. When we reach heaven, and look back from that perspective upon our suffering, we'll agree with the Apostle Paul that it was "our light affliction, which is but for a moment" (2 Cor. 4:17).

These temporary periods of trial are compared by Peter to the purifying process through which raw gold must pass before it reaches its highest value. Our faith needs to be freed from extraneous matter or objectionable elements. This refining is often accomplished only through the fires of affliction. Every Christian, therefore, has the obligation to submit to the hardships of life with a spirit of humility and with a sincere desire of heart to learn from all of them.

Then, when one day we stand before the Saviour, we will find "praise and honor and glory." *Praise*—Jesus Christ will commend us! *Honor*—He will give us a task to perform! *Glory*—He will cause us to shine as sparkling jewels in His kingdom! All the music there will ring out in the major key. But we'll be forever grateful for the minor strains we experienced here on earth, for they will make the heavenly oratorio all the sweeter!

It Is Gloriously Complete
The fourth fact about our great salvation is its glorious completeness. We today, on this side of Calvary, rejoice that we can view clearly what the prophets of the Old Testament saw only in shadowy foreview. For us, the birth, death, and resurrection of Jesus Christ are firmly established facts of history. We have the New Testament Scriptures which record and explain our Saviour's work of redemption. Through faith we have a knowledge and as-

surance unknown to the prophets who lived before Christ. Not even the angels knew then what we know now. Peter declares,

Whom, having not seen, ye love; in whom, though now ye see Him not, yet believing, ye rejoice with joy unspeakable and full of glory, receiving the end of your faith, even the salvation of your souls.

Of which salvation the prophets have inquired and searched diligently, who prophesied of the grace that should come unto you, searching what, or what manner of time the Spirit of Christ who was in them did signify, when He testified beforehand the sufferings of Christ, and the glory that should follow.

Unto whom it was revealed that, not unto themselves but unto us they did minister the things which are now reported unto you by them that have preached the Gospel unto you with the Holy Spirit sent down from heaven, which things the angels desire to look into (1 Peter 1:8-12).

No wonder we can "rejoice with joy unspeakable and full of glory"! We can know with certainty what the prophets could see only dimly, and what is denied to angels. What a comfort this reminder must have been to the suffering believers of Asia Minor! The sacrifice on Calvary had been accomplished; the tomb was empty; the disciples had seen Christ ascend; and they had heard His promise of return!

Based upon the foundation of these redemptive events, no saint should find cause for excessive worry or doubt. The surety of a completed salvation should encourage our hearts, for it brings the hope of eternal glory.

The Truths Applied

To summarize, our great salvation brings a living, well-founded hope, a security based upon God's power, an assurance that gives victory and joy in times of suffering, and a knowledge of spiritual truth exceeding that of angels and the greatest Old Testament saints. But let us also look to Peter and ask, "What shall we do in view of all these blessings? Shall we just sit back and enjoy them?"

His answer is "Never!" Peter describes three responses God expects from us.

First, we should face life squarely without fear. The apostle declared, "Wherefore, gird up the loins of your mind, be sober, and hope to the end for the grace that is to be brought unto you at the revelation of Jesus Christ" (1 Peter 1:13).

In today's terms, Peter is saying, "Get ready for action. Be tough-minded. Face life sensibly and confidently."

We are not to cower in fear, wondering if we can take it and worrying about ourselves. This is not hope at all, but doubt and despair. In periods of hardship or persecution, let's expect to triumph, and determine not to betray the Lord. He'll honor that attitude and strengthen us to meet every demand.

Second, our lives should be marked by obedience. We have been delivered from Satan's kingdom of darkness, and have become members of a new and redeemed humanity. The old way of living, with its selfish and senseless indulgence to natural appetites, is past.

The child of God lives in light, and is called upon to be holy, and to set himself aside for the service of God. Peter writes, "As obedient children, not fashioning yourselves according to the former lusts in your ignorance but, as He who hath called you is holy, so be ye holy in all manner of life, because it is written, 'Be ye holy; for I am holy'" (1 Peter 1:14-16).

True devotion to God expresses itself in holiness. The Lord's perfections become the standard and pattern for our conduct, and we must do our best to live up to them. Let's all take seriously God's statement, "Be ye holy; for I am holy."

The third quality of those who have received God's great salvation is *reverential fear.* God, who is infinitely holy, is the final Judge of every man. He has provided for our salvation at tremendous cost. He gave His Son to be our Saviour. Jesus gained our redemption by shedding His precious blood on the cruel cross. These are holy and awesome truths.

Peter declares, "And if ye call on the Father, who without respect of persons judgeth according to every man's work, pass the time of your *sojourning here in fear*" (1 Peter 1:17). How can we do less than stand in awe of God's great love? It brought us a wonderful salvation! The least we can do in return is walk before Him in joyous optimism, day-by-day obedience, and an attitude of reverential awe, even in the severest persecution.

3

You've Got Change Coming

(1 Peter 1:17-25)

A well-known major league ballplayer, John Hiller, almost died of a coronary, but later returned to star as a relief pitcher for the Detroit Tigers. He said his remarkable recovery came, in part, because he quit smoking, changed eating habits to lose weight, and meticulously followed his doctor's orders. He had known all along that he was overweight and smoking too much, but he didn't think he could do anything about it. When he realized the stakes, however, he had all the incentive he needed. He came back to be named "Fireman of the Year" for the 1973 season.

We're all like him to some degree. We know we should be better persons and improve ourselves, but we lack the information and self-discipline to change. We're just like children, who do not grow up to be well-mannered and responsible young people without a combination of careful teaching, proper motivation, and a helping hand along the way.

The same is true in the spiritual realm. We need

instruction, incentive, and assistance if we are to make progress in the Christian life. All of these ingredients are necessary because it just isn't natural for us to be pure, unselfish, and forgiving. Love somebody the way Jesus loved us? Pray for people who drag our name through the mud? Do good to people who abuse us? "Impossible!" you say. In your own strength, yes. But this is exactly what the Lord expects of us, and He never makes a demand without providing for its fulfillment.

As Peter wrote his first epistle, he perhaps remembered how impossible it was for him to be truly Christlike when he attempted to do it on his own. He very likely recalled how he had failed on the night of the Lord's arrest in Gethsemane. He had been determined to be true to the Lord, and had even boasted that he would never forsake Him. But when the band of men arrested Jesus, Peter fled disgracefully, and by morning had denied his Master three times. But the loving Saviour later restored their broken fellowship, and through the power of the Holy Spirit, Peter became a bold and fearless witness for Christ.

We can well understand why Peter, in view of his own past failure and restoration, would accompany the commands in his letter with specific instruction and the assurance of God's help. When Peter tells the saints to live in reverence, in faith, and in love, each demand is coupled with specific doctrinal truth, and the graciousness of God's provision is emphasized (1 Peter 1:17-25).

Live Reverently

Scripture commands believers to live in reverential awe before God. Peter writes: "And if ye call upon the Father, who without respect of persons judgeth according to every man's work, *pass the time of your sojourning here in fear*" (1 Peter 1:17).

Do not misunderstand the meaning of the phrase *in fear*. In no way does it imply that we are to be terrified of God. We are not to live in dread of Him, like a slave who cowers before a cruel master. Not at all! Rather, the words *in fear* refer to a deep respect for the Lord. We're to stand in awe before His majesty and holiness, and to worship Him as Almighty God. We're to wonder at His mercy and love in providing a way of salvation for us who were "dead in trespasses and sins."

Therefore, Peter says, "live in reverence." He then presents us with two great doctrinal truths to help us understand and obey this command: (1) Believers have the unique privilege of being born into God's family by their faith in the Lord Jesus, and (2) an awful price has been paid to bring us into that family—the shameful death of Jesus Christ, the Son of God.

Our New Relationship

The first great truth to help us live in reverential awe of God is our new relationship with Him as believers in Christ. When we are born again by faith in the Lord Jesus, we enter God's family. Peter is thinking of this when he says that we "call upon the Father."

The Gospel writer John also had this family relationship in mind when he wrote, "But as many as received Him, to them gave He power to become the sons of God, even to them that believe on His name" (John 1:12). Paul, too, alluded to believers as "the children of God" (Rom. 8:16) and as "heirs of God, and joint-heirs with Christ" (v. 17).

As God's children, therefore, we have the privilege of calling Him our heavenly Father. What a blessed relationship! The wonder we feel when we realize we're members of His family gives us a strong incentive to live in reverence before Him.

On the one hand, it gives us assurance and comfort. Just think of it! The Almighty God, who created and sustains the universe, and who is perfect in holiness, loved *us* from all eternity. In spite of our sin, He provided for our redemption. He is now our Father, and His paternal eye is ever upon us. It seems too good to be true! How can we do other than be reverent before a God like this!

On the other hand, with the privilege of being members of God's family comes great responsibility. As children must answer to their fathers, so we are accountable to the Lord. Peter said that God "without respect of persons judgeth according to every man's work." This sobering truth gives us further reason to walk in reverence.

We live a better life when we know we must answer to someone. We're kept from misdeeds we otherwise might commit. In fact, the relationship between our heavenly Father and His children can be compared to that of a loving, high-principled father and his son. This boy will receive instruction in the home and will be disciplined when he does wrong. He will very likely go through life with far more security and much less heartache than his peers whose parents pay no attention to them. The boy may not think about it much, but the guidance he receives brings him much happiness and bolsters his self-image. Yet at the same time he lives under an obligation to do what is right. He knows that if his parents hear reports of wrongdoing on his part, they will rebuke and punish him. Though he may dread going home on some occasions, he is learning to live successfully.

The neglected son, however, often appears to be carefree, and may even taunt the youngster who has the "mean folks." The undisciplined boy can go home with a light heart after being caught in some infraction of the rules because he knows nothing will happen. He'll become increasingly bold, and may even begin breaking the law. But he isn't really happy. He knows that something is missing from his life. In later years, he'll pay the price for his parents' failure.

To summarize, the fact that we can call Almighty God our "Father in heaven," while comforting and assuring, is also awesome in its implications. What condescending love! What incomparable grace! And what a tremendous incentive to live in accordance with His expectations for us and to keep far away from sin!

Salvation's Cost

The second doctrinal basis for a life of reverence is the tremendous price that was paid for our redemption. Peter writes, "Forasmuch as ye know that ye were not redeemed with corruptible things, like silver and gold, from your vain manner of life received by tradition from your fathers, but with the precious blood of Christ, as of a lamb without blemish and without spot" (1 Peter 1:18-19).

The cost of our salvation is immeasurable—the death of God's Son. Jesus Christ died on Calvary to deliver us from the bondage of an empty and unrewarding way of life. Peter referred to it as "your vain manner of life received by tradition from your fathers."

Before we were saved we walked a barren, aimless path that offered neither satisfaction in the present nor hope for the future. We could find little value in the fleeting delights of our materialistic world; for when they faded, our hearts felt hollow and our souls were still troubled.

This sense of futility and emptiness, caused by sin, separates people from God. Even highly successful men and women are often wretched and despairing, not knowing that their deepest need is for a right relationship with the Lord. Multitudes, enslaved to drink, gambling, tobacco, hallucinatory drugs, or gross perversion, are unaware that this "vain manner of life" into which they fall so naturally is the result of their estrangement from God. How true the famous prayer of Augustine, "Thou hast made us for Thyself, and our souls are restless until they find their rest in Thee."

From an empty life alienated from God and marked by sin and guilt, we have been emancipated, as the apostle points out, by the "blood of Christ" (v. 19). This blood is *precious*, worth far more than gold and silver or any of earth's corruptible treasures.

Peter also refers to Jesus as "the lamb without blemish and without spot." He was undoubtedly thinking of the Passover lamb, still a part of Jewish religious life.

The story of the Passover is recorded in Exodus 12. The people of Israel had been subjected to cruel slavery. The Egyptian ruler refused to let the Israelites go, and God sent severe plagues upon the land. The tenth plague brought death to the first-born son in every family. On that memorable night, before the angel of death came to each home, the Israelites were to kill a lamb and sprinkle its blood on the doorposts and lintels of their houses. The death angel then passed by every blood-sprinkled dwelling.

The Passover lamb, which had to be without

blemish, was a type or symbol of the Lord Jesus. He, "who knew no sin," was made "to be sin for us," delivering us from the power of death and bringing us to God (see 2 Cor. 5:21).

Christian friend, do you reflect upon the depths of despair and sin from which you were delivered? Do you marvel that God gave His Son to the shame and agony of Calvary for your redemption? What thrilling thoughts to contemplate! How uplifting and moving! What incentives to a life of continual reverence before God!

A consciousness of the Lord and His holiness doesn't come naturally. We are born with a nature that is self-centered, and this tendency remains with us even after we are saved. But when we realize that we are God's children, and that His Son paid the full price for our salvation, the Holy Spirit uses these blessed truths to help us do the impossible.

Live in Faith

The second obligation of a child of God is to live believingly. We are saved through our faith in Jesus Christ, and the continuing Christian life is one of trust. Peter, speaking of Christ, says, "Who verily was foreordained before the foundation of the world, but was manifest in these last times for you, who by Him do *believe in God*, who raised Him up from the dead and gave Him glory, *that your faith and hope might be in God*" (1 Peter 1:20-21).

In these verses Peter is speaking of the day-by-day trust that is the essence of godly living, not the act of faith at the time of salvation. This is indicated first in the words "who by Him do believe *in* God," for the Greek preposition is *eis*, which usually describes a continuous relationship. These early believers were living daily a life of humble trust in

God. This unceasing belief is also in the apostle's mind when he says that God raised Jesus "that your faith and hope might be *in* [*eis*] God." The resurrection of Christ, therefore, makes possible a life of continuing faith and hope in God. We know we serve a risen Saviour, and this encourages unwavering trust, and keeps the prospect of future glory ever before us.

Peter again couples our responsibility with important doctrinal teaching to give us instruction and help. He refers to two fundamental truths which form the basis of our abiding life of faith: (1) Our salvation is grounded in God's eternal plan. (2) The resurrection of Jesus Christ is the guarantee that the price for sin has been paid in full and that the power of death has been completely broken.

Planned from Eternity

We are comforted to realize that our redemption is not based upon a last-minute decision of God to send His Son to redeem us. It was actually planned long before the worlds were created. Peter says that Christ "was foreordained before the foundation of the world, but was manifest in these last times for you" (1 Peter 1:20). In the eternal counsels of God, the fall of man was foreseen, a way of redemption was planned, and those who would be saved were chosen. Then, in the fullness of time, the eternal Son of the Father entered the world through the virgin birth to be our substitute in life and in death, thus fulfilling God's will to the very letter.

Therefore, the suffering Christians of Asia Minor had no reason to doubt God's goodness, even in seasons of adversity and persecution. Surely He who planned their redemption and gave His Son to die for their sins would not desert them now!

After all, they had the glorious privilege of living

on the sunny side of Calvary. Peter tells them that Christ "was manifest in these last times for you." The Old Testament believers presented sacrifices which only prefigured the cross. As New Testament saints, however, the believers of Asia Minor could rejoice in the knowledge that Jesus had come, and that He had already paid the penalty for all sin. Surely we, too, can trust in the God who is carrying out His eternal plan for our good, and who has proven His love by the gift of His Son.

Demonstrated in Resurrection

The second encouraging truth set forth to help believers live in continual trust is the resurrected life of Christ. The apostle said that the Father "raised Him [Christ] up from the dead and gave Him glory, that your faith and hope might be in God" (1 Peter 1:21).

The New Testament teaches that the resurrection of the Lord Jesus is proof that God was completely satisfied with His Son's sacrifice for sinners. That's why the risen Christ appeared to His disciples so often. He could have risen from the grave and gone directly to the Father without anybody ever seeing Him. The empty tomb would have given powerful, mute witness of His resurrection, and the descent of the Holy Spirit on Pentecost would have been adequate evidence that Jesus had really returned to heaven. But God made the evidences of the resurrection public to give us additional proof.

How strengthening, when all seems to be going wrong, to reflect upon the inspired statement, "But now is Christ risen from the dead and become the firstfruits of them that slept" (1 Cor. 15:26). Oh, that empty tomb of the first Easter morning! How wonderful its message! What an encouragement, that "our faith and hope might be in God."

Live in Love

Peter's third appeal is for love-filled lives on the part of God's people. He writes, "Seeing that ye have purified your souls in obeying the truth through the Spirit unto unfeigned love of the brethren, see that ye love one another with a pure heart fervently" (1 Peter 1:22).

The word *love* appears twice in this passage. In the original Greek, two different words are used. The apostle speaks first of *phileō* love, a warm feeling of affection, and second of *agapaō* love, a completely selfless concern for the welfare of others. He assumes that these first-century believers already possess a mutual fondness for one another [*phileō* love], and challenges them to the pure, fervent *agapaō* love that willingly sacrifices one's own interests.

Our Spiritual Cleansing

First, let us consider the genuine affection believers feel for one another as brothers and sisters in Christ. Note that this is a result of their spiritual cleansing: "ye have *purified your souls* in obeying the truth through the Spirit *unto unfeigned love of the brethren*" (v. 22). The Greek words translated "unfeigned love" are *philadelphian anupokriton,* and denote a "sincere, brotherly, heart-devotion." The apostle declares that they possess this kind of love right now, and says it is based upon a spiritual cleansing they share.

Some difference of opinion exists as to just what he means by the phrase, *ye have purified your souls in obeying the truth.* Certain Bible students, taking these words to refer to the cleansing Christians receive at their salvation, believe the apostle is saying that these early Christians purified their souls *when they believed the Gospel.* Of course, it is God who does the forgiving and the work of cleansing, but they claim that Peter is referring to man's responsibility in salvation, emphasizing the fact that they obeyed the word of truth when they heard it.

A number of passages in the New Testament speak of believing the Gospel as an act of obedience (see Acts 6:7; 2 Thes. 1:8; Rom. 6:17; 10:16). Some, therefore, take Peter's words, "Seeing that ye have purified your souls in obeying the truth . . . unto unfeigned love of the brethren," as a reference to the spiritual cleansing all who believe on Christ receive at the very moment of salvation. And this common experience is recognized by them as the basis for that special feeling of affection, the *phileō* love, we have toward our brothers and sisters in Christ.

Other commentators, however, maintain that the purification of soul and obedience to the truth referred to in verse 22 took place some time after salvation. They say that some of the early Christians of Asia Minor may have drifted back to their old unsaved friends rather than continuing in fellowship with the saints, but that now they had changed their ways. Kenneth Wuest expressed this view as follows:

> Now, the thing that caused some of these Christians to revert to their former worldly associates was failure to obey the Word of God. Consequently, their heart-life became sinful. Therefore, they preferred their former sinful companions to their fellow Christians. But when they started to obey the Word again, their souls were purified, and they came to have that fondness and affection for the Christian brethren which is the normal condition among saints who are living lives of obedience

to God's Word. The love which they showed toward other believers was an unassumed one. It came from the heart.*

Whether the experience of cleansing in obedience to the truth occurred at the moment of salvation, or at some later time, it created a sincere fondness for brothers and sisters in Christ. Have you ever noticed how a special affinity rises in your heart for a stranger when you see him pray before he eats in a restaurant? Or when you hear a person speak a word of testimony for Christ in a public place? Or when you hear reports of believers being dreadfully persecuted because of their faith? Just realizing that every person who believes on the Lord Jesus is a forgiven sinner like you, and is going to the same heaven, should make you sense a oneness with him.

Our Spiritual Birth

Having dealt with the *phileo* kind of love among believers, the apostle challenges his readers to *agapao* love. He connects it with the new birth. We read, "See that ye love one another with a pure heart fervently, being born again" (1 Peter 1:22-23).

This is a call for the kind of love which rejoices when good things happen to people, even though we may not naturally like these people. It means sacrificing valuable time or giving generously of scarce commodities. It calls for sharing the sorrows of people whose attitudes and actions ordinarily are distasteful to us. It means praying for those who may oppose us, turning the other cheek, going the extra mile, and actually sacrificing our own desires to help the other person. It goes far beyond mere affection for fellow believers.

---

* Kenneth S. Wuest, *First Peter in the Greek New Testament* (Grand Rapids, Mich.: Wm. B. Eerdmans Publishing Company, 1942), p. 46.

By nature we are sinful and selfish, and to live in *agapaō* love is impossible in our own strength. Peter realized this full well, and therefore called attention to God's work of regeneration, which is shared by every believer. Immediately after issuing the command for fervent *agapē* love, he writes, "Being born again." The miracle of the new birth gives us the capacity to love purely and unselfishly. Because God has implanted new life within us, we have the potential to live above the ordinary. Failure comes when we do not avail ourselves of the provision the Lord has made for us.

After mentioning the new birth, the apostle moves logically to a glowing soliloquy about the Word of God, which is used by the Holy Spirit to bring us new life.

> Being born again, not of corruptible seed, but of incorruptible, by the Word of God, which liveth and abideth forever. For all flesh is like grass, and all the glory of man like the flower of grass. The grass withereth, and its flower falleth away, but the Word of the Lord endureth forever. And this is the Word which by the Gospel is preached unto you (1 Peter 1:23-25).

I'm glad the apostle quoted Isaiah's promise that God's Word will outlast the passing elements of our natural world. The grass of the field dies quickly. Flowers last only a little while. Human life is but a brief span. The Word of God, however, continues to abide generation after generation, and through the ages of eternity.

You see, sometimes we don't feel as if we are "born again." There are times when we fail to love others as we ought. But when we become discouraged, we are reminded that our salvation is grounded in the infallible, unchanging, and incorruptible Word of God.

Summary

As we conclude this section of Peter's letter, let's review Peter's practical exhortations and related doctrinal truths for "doing the impossible." First, *live reverently*. Let every day be marked by reflecting upon God's salvation and the cost involved.

Second, *live believingly*. Take seriously the biblical affirmation that your salvation was in God's plan from all eternity, and that His complete satisfaction with Christ's sacrifice has been amply demonstrated.

Third, *live lovingly*. Learn to appropriate the wonderful truth of your new life in Christ. As a born-again person, you are enabled by the indwelling Holy Spirit to achieve a degree of love far beyond your natural inclinations. He will help you to turn the other cheek, and to pray for those who may disagree with you, and to seek the welfare of others even above your own.

You will then begin "doing the impossible."

4

The How Is in the Who

(1 Peter 2:1-10)

All of us have times when we feel the need for self-improvement. Let's face it, we're never completely satisfied with ourselves as we are. We may wish to better our appearance, so we decide to lose a few pounds, get our teeth fixed, or do something about our hair. We may be unhappy with our behavior, so we try to overcome a tendency to be irritable or impatient. Or, we may dislike certain habits we've fallen into, such as staying up late every night or watching too much television.

Some people fight a far more desperate battle with themselves. They are compulsive spenders, or gamblers, or have become enslaved to alcohol or hallucinatory drugs. Others are unfaithful in marriage, or become uncontrollably angry and inflict painful physical injury upon members of their family.

But whether the source of dissatisfaction with self involves something minor such as our appearance, or a major moral problem that brings harm to ourselves and our loved ones, we all know that significant changes are not made easily. It takes discipline, effort, and sacrifice. Indeed, most people seem unable to break their bad habits.

A number of organizations have been established to help people overcome their weaknesses so that they may lead more happy and productive lives. These programs have achieved a measure of success, but even their most enthusiastic proponents admit that they cannot produce radical inner changes in people. They merely enable people to strengthen their willpower by following a prescribed set of guidelines and by scrupulously avoiding things which might trigger another fall. The alcoholic, for example, is advised to stay out of taverns and refuse that first drink. He must still think of himself as an alcoholic, and not claim that he has been cured of his drinking problem. Only his behavior has been altered.

The Gospel of Jesus Christ, on the other hand, goes far beyond all human efforts. It's not just "behavior modification" or the acquisition of a new life-style, but the introduction of a complete inner change. The Bible speaks of this transformation as the "new birth." At the moment of conversion, the believer in Christ is given a brand new nature. He's regenerated—"born again."

The new Christian is not to remain a spiritual infant, however, but to grow into a mature, confident disciple of Christ. The apostle, addressing the believers in Asia Minor as "newborn babes," encouraged them to take three positive steps for spiritual growth: (1) renounce sin, (2) feed on God's Word, and (3) understand and accept their place in God's plan (1 Peter 2:1-10). This is good advice for *all* Christians, so as we consider each step, I trust you'll check out your own life.

Renounce Sin

The first step is to renounce once-for-all the sins of your old life. Peter wrote, "Wherefore, laying aside all malice, and all guile, and hypocrisies, and envies, and all evil speakings" (1 Peter 2:1). The Greek participle translated "laying aside" in this verse is *apothemenoi,* and is a command for decisive action. Believers must resolutely put aside the sins mentioned here. The word means literally "to strip off," or "to throw hastily aside," as you would a garment if it were on fire or saturated with a powerful acid.

Men of Jesus' day often wore long, flowing robes. Suppose a man were to stand too close to a fire and suddenly discover his clothing ablaze. What would he do? He would strip it off and throw it aside. That's exactly what Peter meant for us to do with the sins of the old nature.

In this passage, five specific sins are singled out which should never characterize the life of a Christian: malice, guile, hypocrisy, envy, and gossip. As we "grow in grace," we're to leave these evils behind as part of the old way of life.

The first sin is *malice.* The Greek term for malice is *kakia,* often used as a summary word for evil in general, but sometimes for a deep-seated hatred of others, stemming from a basic selfishness. In a sense, all sin originates from the single fountainhead of self-love.

On some occasions, this selfishness leads to deep, dark feelings of intense animosity. We hate others so much we want to hurt them. We're somehow not satisfied until we make them suffer. How contrary this is to the principle of love for our fellowman, and especially our brothers and sisters in Christ, as taught in the Bible! Malice, wishing others harm, should be stripped off as soon as we enter God's family. If you are harboring ill will toward anyone, or wishing them misfortune, let me urge you to renounce this sin right now. It has no place in your Christian life—for any reason!

The second sin which we must rip off like a burning garment is *guile*. This term comes from the Greek word *dolos,* and refers to clever or tricky practices. In its verb form it means "to deceive" or "to catch with bait." Guile is the clever manipulation of people to serve one's own ends. A person is guilty of this sin when he misquotes someone in order to hurt him, makes misleading statements about him, utilizes innuendo, or resorts to other underhanded methods to bring harm. No believer should ever stoop to doing such things.

The Lord Jesus Himself set the standard. Though people lied about Him, tried in every way possible to trick Him into self-incriminating statements, and even abused Him physically, He never once retorted in kind. In fact, Peter used the same word in verse 22 of this chapter to describe our Lord's exemplary conduct, saying that He "did no sin, neither was *guile* found in His mouth."

The third fault to be renounced is *hypocrisy*. Peter says, "Wherefore, laying aside . . . hypocrisies." The root of the word translated "hypocrisies" traces its origin to Greek law. Men who were appointed to answer legal questions or render judgments stood behind a screen or wore a mask so that people would not know their identities. Later on, in religious festivals, the choirs from various city-states enacted simple dramas, with one individual standing out from the chorus and answering in solo to what the others chanted. Wearing a mask, either comic or tragic, he would really become an actor. Through the use of a costume, he was transformed into either a most noble character or one of extreme cruelty and degradation. The actor, playing a role not really his true self, was called a *hupokritēs*.

In time, the term "hypocrite" became a designation for anyone whose words and actions did not reflect his true identity or feelings. Today we use it to describe a person who greets you with a smile when he actually hates you; one who appears to be a friend but is only using you to gain power or prestige. We also use this word when speaking of someone who seems to be pious but actually thinks only of himself.

The old country preacher may not have used the best grammar, but he certainly was on target when he told his congregation, "Be what you are and not what you ain't; because if you ain't what you are, then you are what you think you ain't."

The fourth sin Peter tells us to cast aside is *envy*. This is a feeling of discontent and jealousy such as arises when another person has greater talents or possessions, or receives more honors than we. Envy has sometimes been described as a "mental cancer," because it gradually destroys spiritual health. The Bible tells us that this was the sin that prompted Joseph's brothers to cast him into a pit and sell him as a slave. It was also the root cause of the rebellion of Aaron and Miriam against their brother Moses. In the New Testament, Pilate was aware of the fact that the Jewish leaders were calling for the death of Jesus because of envy (see Matt. 27:18).

Envy has broken friendships by the thousands, has destroyed the effective witness of numerous churches, and has been one of the most significant causes of blighted lives. That's why people often refer to it as the "green-eyed monster." Scripture terms it "rottenness of the bones" (Prov. 14:30).

Envy always arises because of thinking more of oneself than another, and it has no place in the life of a child of God.

The fifth transgression specifically listed by Peter is *evil speaking*. This is a reference to slander, often spread in the form of careless or intentional gossip. Anytime we discredit or belittle someone, we are committing this sin. Whenever we pass on to someone a negative or scandalous story, we are guilty of this evil. Let's be on guard against this misuse of the tongue, for it violates the Christian principles of love and truth.

Christian, you have been born into God's family, and He wants you to grow. The first step is to renounce, to strip off the sins of the old life, especially malice, guile, hypocrisy, envy, and slander. You may not gain complete victory over them immediately. After all, you don't grow from infancy to adulthood overnight. But when you acknowledge these sins to be incompatible with a good Christian testimony and determine in your heart to overcome them by the Spirit's power, you have made the right beginning.

Feed Upon God's Word

The second requisite for growth in the Christian life is a hunger for the Word of God. This will lead a believer to study and learn from the Bible. Peter charged, "As newborn babes, desire the pure milk of the Word, that ye may grow by it" (1 Peter 2:2).

A healthy baby has a natural desire for milk, and he grows when he drinks enough of it. Spiritual growth comes just as naturally for every believer who partakes of the "soul food" found in the Bible. What a tragedy that some Christians remain spiritual infants all their lives because they never feed upon the truths of Scripture!

Peter says that Christians should desire the "*pure milk of the Word.*" This means that it must be unadulterated, free from all impurities. If a person goes to a church where biblical truth is watered down by liberalism, he will suffer malnutrition. An individual who hears teaching from a cult which denies the doctrines of the Trinity, the deity of Christ, or the substitutionary nature of Christ's death on the cross may actually be slowly dying of poison.

Read the Bible for yourself, and ask the Holy Spirit for guidance. He will lead you aright (see John 16:13; 1 John 2:27). You will receive added help from men of God who have been given special gifts, but the Bible is to be your basic textbook. Then, attend a church in which the truths of the Word of God are believed and taught. The combination of sound, biblical preaching and personal Bible study leads to confidence, holiness, and maturity.

Accept God's Plan

The third step in spiritual growth is the intelligent grasp of God's purpose in this age for the Church and for the individual. We were not born again to flounder aimlessly, having no direction or goal. God has a detailed plan for us, and we must accept and understand our place in it. Three practical truths, discernible in 1 Peter 2:5-11, will help you mature as a believer in Christ. (1) You must see yourself as one of a great company of believers, the Church. (2) You are to present your life totally to God as a spiritual sacrifice. (3) Your life is to bring praise and honor to God.

A Member of Christ's Body

Every growing Christian must realize that even though salvation is an individual matter, the believer does not live as a solitary being. He is a member of the Church, the Body of Christ. Peter compares our role in the Church to bricks in a building: "Ye also, as living stones, are built up a spiritual house" (1 Peter 2:5). As "living stones" we are part of a great spiritual edifice being constructed by God. Every brick or stone of the structure is needed, but not one manifests its true value standing by itself.

Every individual stone in any building, no matter what its position, is important. The absence of even one brick would leave an unsightly hole, and would be noticed immediately. All the planning and designing would go to waste, for the aesthetic effect would be ruined. The structure would also be weakened, and other flaws might soon develop.

In the Church, the spiritual house being built by God, each individual has a distinct and unique place to fill. Paul taught the same truth, using different imagery, when he compared the Church to a human body and the individuals to its members (see Rom. 12:3-8; 1 Cor. 12:4-31). Every believer has his own work to do in the Church. God looks upon the one performing the most menial tasks with just as much delight as He does the one who receives the plaudits of men. Rewards will be given on the basis of faithfulness, not accomplishment. A working man who goes calling and witnesses faithfully may receive a greater reward than a minister who has achieved international recognition.

Christianity is a community. We are not to isolate ourselves from our fellow believers. Notice the use of collective nouns: "But ye are a chosen *generation,* a royal *priesthood,* an holy *nation,* a *people* of His own" (1 Peter 2:9). We are part of the collective body of Christ, and this should be a powerful incentive for us to pray for and work with our fellow believers.

A Spiritual Sacrifice

In the plan of God for His children we are not only members of the Church universal, we are also called to be priests. "Ye also, as living stones, are built up a spiritual house, *an holy priesthood.* . . . But ye are a chosen generation, *a royal priesthood,* an holy nation, a people of His own" (1 Peter 2:5, 9).

Peter is not telling us that we are to present animal sacrifices, as did the priests of the Old Testament. That entire system ended when Jesus died on the cross to pay the price for our sin. Rather we are to offer ourselves to the Lord in complete dedication and service. Paul expressed this truth as follows, "I beseech you therefore, brethren, by the mercies of God, that ye present your bodies a living sacrifice, holy, acceptable unto God, which is your reasonable service" (Rom. 12:1).

As "a royal priesthood," we're to give ourselves completely to the Lord. Our bodies, our minds, our abilities, our potentialities are all to be turned over to Him. Everything we do every day of our lives is to be offered up to the Lord. Our times of worship, our working hours at the office or factory, our recreation and time at home—wherever we go and whatever we do, we belong to Him. Sometimes ministers and missionaries are said to be in "full-time Christian work," but this can be misleading. Every believer should consider God's service his main purpose in life.

One reason churches sometimes fail to make an impact upon the community is that they are filled with "part-time" Christians, people who appear dedicated and pious on Sunday morning but seem to set aside their Christianity during the week. It is impossible to witness to a man after you've lied to him about a car you are selling him, or to invite a neighbor to church after a gossip session. Inconsistency is a mark of spiritual immaturity, and one of the indispensable factors in Christian growth is unreserved and uninterrupted presentation of oneself to God.

A Voice of Praise

Peter concludes this section with a final duty we are to perform as part of God's plan. He said that we are to "show forth the praises of Him who hath called [us] out of darkness into His marvelous light" (1 Peter 2:9). We once were controlled by Satan, the "god of this age," and walked in the darkness of sin. Guilt and condemnation weighed heavily upon us, and we were helpless and afraid. But then one day we met the Saviour by faith, and He who is the Light flooded our soul with His eternal love and grace. We were instantaneously reborn, made citizens of heaven, and recipients of His new life.

Now, as believers in God, we are to testify to His greatness and goodness. As Peter said, we must "show forth the praises of Him who hath called" us. The word "praises" is a translation of the Greek *aretas*, which means "eminent qualities" or "excellencies." The apostle has in mind here the beauties and perfections of God as they are made known to men. We experienced in our salvation, for example, God's love and grace and power. Now, as "heirs of God, and joint-heirs with Christ" (Rom. 8:17), we should so live that the qualities of our heavenly Father shine forth from our lives, giving witness to His glory and grace.

Every time we break a sinful habit, show consideration for those in need, or react in love to our enemies, we're bringing honor to God. Faithful attendance at church, honesty in business, harmony in the home, and patience with the children show forth His praise. The result will be that men and women lost in spiritual darkness will come to know Christ, the Light of the world, through our witness.

In conclusion, God's salvation has brought you new life, and He expects you to grow. To do so, you must renounce sin, feed on God's Word, and accept your place and responsibility in God's plan. If you are a healthy, growing, vibrant Christian, you will indeed "show forth the praises of Him who hath called you out of darkness into His marvelous light." The world will then be able to see the wonderful power, love, and grace of God in and through you.

If you are a Christian, are you maturing spiritually? Is the growth process a reality in your life? If not, renounce, strip off, cast aside the sins of the old life. Study the Word. Get involved in the work of a Bible-believing church. Present yourself to the Lord for service. Then, determine with God's help to bring honor to His name.

5

It's Your Right to Be Wronged

(1 Peter 2:11-25)

"We demand our rights!" It seems we're hearing statements such as this all the time. It is the theme of impassioned speeches on the floor of the United Nations. It's the cry of minority groups and women's lib organizations. It's the rallying call of labor unions and big business, and is used to justify crippling strikes and uncalled-for price increases. The spirit behind this cry most clearly embodies the thinking of today's world, and expresses in sharp detail man's sinful and selfish nature.

The Lord Jesus taught a completely opposite view of life. He said, "The last shall be first, and the first last" (Matt. 20:16). Christ Himself, on the night before His crucifixion, set the pattern by assuming a servant's role and washing His disciples' feet. The writers of the epistles, in addition, continually used words such as *obey, submit,* and *yield.* Throughout the entire Bible, believers are instructed to adopt an attitude of humility and submission.

But what if a Christian is arrested on false charges? Is he still to be submissive? Of course, a

55

believer has every right to insist upon due process of law, but somehow the spirit he manifests must be completely different from those who demand, "I want my rights."

The Apostle Peter, who had learned many lessons along the way in his own Christian experience, was writing to believers living under difficult conditions. Many of them were counted among the 60 million slaves of that day, and wondered who they should put first—their masters or Christ. Even people with the full rights of citizenship were in trouble, for the Roman emperor had initiated a widespread program of persecution.

Vital questions had arisen, therefore, concerning the Christian's relationship to those in authority over him. Peter confronted this issue in his first epistle, answering five questions facing these believers: (1) Who has authority over me? (2) What is the extent of my obligation to obey? (3) Why must I be submissive? (4) What must I do when I am unjustly treated? (5) How can I fulfill my obligation in a truly Christlike spirit? The apostle provides specific answers to each of these questions (1 Peter 2:11-25).

To Whom Must I Submit?

We know that governmental authority begins with the top official of the country, encompasses congressmen and governors, reaches down to mayors, and even includes the part-time deputy sheriff. A high-salaried individual who directs a large corporation might wonder, "Must I be submissive when a policeman who makes less than a tenth of my salary stops me and issues me a speeding ticket I don't deserve?"

Peter leaves no room for uncertainty. He writes, "Submit yourselves to *every ordinance of man* for the Lord's sake, whether it be to the king, as supreme, or unto governors, as unto them that are sent by him for the punishment of evildoers, and for the praise of them that do well" (1 Peter 2: 13-14). The expression *every ordinance of man* means that we are to obey *all* the laws of *every* branch of government, including those controlling traffic and relating to the income tax. Sorry about that! But Peter was writing under the inspiration of the Holy Spirit, and we have no right to object.

If as Christians we take Peter seriously, we will try to observe all ordinances and laws, even when we question their value or wisdom. If the sign says "35 miles per hour," we won't be driving as fast as we want, keeping a sharp lookout for speed traps or police cruisers. Neither will we cheat on our income tax returns, nor find ways to get around real estate regulations or other legal restrictions. We'll accept the laws as pertaining to us, and obey them to the best of our ability.

Peter goes further than discussing our obligation to civil authorities and laws, for he also includes the employee's responsibility to his employer. "Servants, be subject to your masters with all fear; not only to the good and gentle but also to the perverse" (1 Peter 2:18).

The word *servants* in this verse refers to slaves. The apostle commands Christian slaves to obey their masters even when they make unfair demands. It isn't that God approves of slavery. Not at all! In fact, history has proven that when the principles of the Bible are followed, slavery is abolished. But in New Testament days, when it was still in practice, the Christian slave was to follow his new Master in his attitude toward the man who owned him.

This principle of submission applies in the employer-employee relationship as well. Authority must be recognized and maintained on all levels of society if we are to live in order, harmony, and productivity. The believer in the Lord Jesus, knowing that God loves humility, unselfishness, and obedience, is to set the example.

Let us apply this to our modern day. A believer in Christ is to respect all authority, obeying every rule of his government. He will do his best to meet his employer's demands. He is not to be a rebel, an agitator, or call for civil disobedience. This does not mean he must condone a despotic, dishonest regime. Nor should he be silent in the face of injustice or unfair social conditions. In a democracy he should actively support efforts to bring about good government. But his manner of speech and action must always reflect a sincere respect for authority.

What Is the Extent of My Obligation?
What are Christians to do if obedience to the laws of authorities would mean breaking God's commandments? What if a government official asks you to tell a lie for him? What if an employer orders you to do something dishonest? In situations like this, you must put God's will before that of man.

Peter knew by experience what it is to be forced to choose between doing the will of the Lord and obeying the demands of human authority. Shortly after Pentecost, the rulers in Jerusalem commanded Peter and John "not to speak at all nor teach in the name of Jesus" (Acts 4:18). But the apostles kept right on preaching until they were arrested. Dragged before the tribunal, they were asked, "Did not we strictly command you that ye should not teach in this name?" (Acts 5:28)

The apostles replied, "We ought to obey God rather than men" (Acts 5:29). Forced to make a choice between a clear command from Christ and an order from human authorities, they rendered obedience to God. *He* is the ultimate authority.

But let me remind you that noncompliance with government regulations is proper only when obeying them would clearly violate God's law. I may disagree with a 25-mile-per-hour limit on a little-traveled highway, but this gives me no right to go any faster. I may be convinced that a certain tax is not fair, but I must "render to Caesar the things that are Caesar's." I may have good reason to believe a public official is dishonest or unqualified, but this gives me no right to advocate disobedience to him or his department. As a child of God, I must keep the laws.

At this juncture the apostle felt it necessary to outline our relationships with our fellowmen in general. He presents this summary statement: "Honor all men. Love the brotherhood. Fear God. Honor the king" (1 Peter 2:17).

First, you and I are to "honor all men." Every human being is made in the image of God and is a candidate for His redeeming grace. In apostolic days, when a wealthy man became a Christian, "honor all men" meant he had to adjust his thinking regarding slaves. As believers today we have no right to despise anyone, though we may be shocked and revolted by the actions of some people. In short, the child of God is never to look upon another person with contempt. The apostle said, "Honor all men."

The second brief command is, "Love the brotherhood," our brothers and sisters in Christ. Yes, we who know the Lord Jesus must honor all men, but we are to go beyond that in totally unselfish love for our fellow-believers. After all, we have been united in a common faith, we possess a common hope, and we share a common desire to do the will of God. The consciousness of our oneness in Christ makes possible a sincere, abiding love for the brotherhood.

The third imperative is, "Fear God." As noted earlier, this means believers are to live in reverential awe of the Lord. The Bible declares, "The fear of the Lord is the beginning of knowledge" (Prov. 1:7). When a person reveres God, he will see all of life in proper focus. He will also be given a powerful incentive to obey the Lord, even when it might result in suffering at the hands of men.

The fourth command is, "Honor the king." Peter's use of the present imperative, which could be translated, "Continue showing honor to the emperor," may be significant. Some of the believers in Asia Minor were very likely speaking scornfully about Nero. He was already persecuting believers and showing signs of becoming a monster of iniquity. The Christians, however, were to honor him even though they couldn't admire him.

This is always timely advice! The Watergate episode and other scandals have caused many to downgrade their concept of public officials, but as Christians we are to give honor to our leaders even when we are heartsick about their morals. The Bible demands that we recognize all rulers as bearing authority by God's decree. Paul declares, "Let every soul be subject unto the higher powers. For there is no power but of God; the powers that be are ordained of God" (Rom. 13:1).

The state, therefore, is an instrument in the hand of God to preserve the world from chaos. Every political leader, whether he believes in God or repudiates Him, has been given authority to prevent total anarchy, an evil even worse than oppression. That's why we have been commanded to obedience.

Dr. Paul Rees tells the story of the martyrdom of Genesius during the reign of the cruel Roman emperor Diocletian, to illustrate the twin injunctions, "Fear God" and "Honor the king." Genesius had been brought up in a Christian home, but had rejected Christ. An actor, he stood in the center of the arena, pantomiming a Christian baptism to entertain the emperor. Suddenly he stopped and shouted, "I want to receive the grace of Christ, that I may be born again. I want to be set free from the sins which have been my ruin!" He then turned toward Diocletian, who was sitting in his regal box in the stands, and cried, "Illustrious Emperor, and all of you who have laughed loudly at this parody, believe me! Christ is the true King!" The Roman sovereign became livid with anger and ordered Genesius to be ripped with claws, burned with torches, and beheaded. Just before his death, this valiant believer cried out, "There is no king except Christ, whom I have seen and whom I worship. For Him I would die a thousand times. I am sorry for my sin, and becoming so late a soldier of the true King."

What was it that led Genesius to receive Jesus Christ as Saviour, and to confess Him openly even though he knew it would result in death? It was the fear of God. The Christian training of his childhood had made an impact, and now, under the convicting work of the Holy Spirit, his reverence for God made it impossible to finish his blasphemous parody. But he still honored the king. That's why he spoke no foul or derogatory word, saying respectfully, "Illustrious Emperor." He feared God, and he honored the king.

Why Be Submissive?

Why does God put so much emphasis on submission? Just why is it important to obey all government authorities, even honoring people we feel don't really deserve it? Peter gives us the answer: "For so is the will of God, that with well-doing ye may put to silence the ignorance of foolish men; as free, and not using your liberty for a cloak of maliciousness, but as the servants of God" (1 Peter 2:15-16). By submitting to all authorities, believers leave the critics of Christ and His people with nothing to say.

Now, the natural thing to do when irresponsible and unfounded accusations are made against us is to rise up in self-defense. If this doesn't work, we find a way to retaliate. But God does not expect such conduct from His children! We must resist the impulse to overreact. Our self-restraint will deprive the enemy of new grounds for criticism. The Christian way to muzzle false accusers is to manifest the spirit of Christ, and to continue obeying all laws and showing respect for all authorities.

Peter goes on to say, "As free, and not using your liberty as a cloak of maliciousness, but as the servants of God" (v. 16). This reminds us that we, as believers, are free from *total* subjection to any man. We have been made citizens of heaven, and are the subjects of Him who is Lord of lords and King of kings. But we must not use this great spiritual liberty as an excuse for malicious deeds. As the bondslaves of God, we will submit to human authority "for the Lord's sake."

This truth has significant implications for us today. Every believer has a high and worthy motive for submission to civil authority—obedience to God. We do not obey only because we fear punishment by earthly rulers—this would place us in the category of slaves. We submit to authority, even when human leaders are oppressive and unfair, because we know it is what the Lord wants.

What Must I Do When Treated Unjustly?

Most believers are more than happy to obey authorities when they believe their demands are reasonable and fair. But what if a Christian is mistreated? Peter tells us what our attitude should be: "For this is thankworthy, if a man for conscience toward God endure grief, suffering wrongfully. For what glory is it if, when ye are buffeted for your faults, ye shall take it patiently? But if, when you do well and suffer for it, ye take it patiently, this is acceptable with God" (1 Peter 2:19-20).

When we are abused, we must "take it patiently." As we do, we show forth one of the unique glories of our Christian faith, the wonder of God's grace. Peter's words, "For this is thankworthy," literally mean, "For this is grace."

Having stated our obligation, Peter points us to Jesus Christ as our model. He writes, "For even hereunto were ye called, because Christ also suffered for us, *leaving us an example,* that ye should follow His steps; who did no sin, neither was guile found in His mouth; who, when He was reviled, reviled not again; when He suffered, He threatened not, but committed Himself to Him that judgeth righteously" (1 Peter 2:21-23).

Jesus suffered *blamelessly.* He had done nothing to deserve the terrible treatment He received, for He "did no sin, neither was guile found in His mouth." We too should live above reproach.

Our Lord also suffered *graciously.* Remembering our Lord's patient endurance in the long hours of

His humiliation, Peter wrote, "When He [Jesus] was reviled, [He] reviled not again; when He suffered, He threatened not." The Saviour did not react bitterly. No words of contempt for His enemies escaped His lips. He did not curse His executioners. And when we are buffeted, we should follow His example.

In addition, our Saviour suffered *trustfully*, for Peter says He "committed Himself to Him that judgeth righteously." We too must turn ourselves over to our heavenly Father, even as Jesus did. His promises will not fail.

Yes, when we are maltreated, we must "take it patiently." Like our Saviour, we must suffer blamelessly, graciously, and trustfully. The Lord Jesus set the example, and He did so, not only for servants who are abused by unkind masters, but for all His children when they are hated and persecuted.

Millions of oppressed Christians through the centuries have made Christ their model, suffering blamelessly, without retaliation, and in faith. Even today, in China, North Korea, North Vietnam, and Chad, followers of Christ are being tortured and put to death. Only God knows the full story, but from the information that has leaked out we know that many have obeyed Peter's admonition to "take it patiently." They have faced terrible torment with an attitude that has amazed even their bitterest enemies.

How Can I Fulfill My Obligation?
Even though we know what we ought to do when oppressed, we must still face the question, "How can I find the strength to follow the Lord's demands?" Peter answers the question for us, writing, "Who [Christ] His own self bore our sins in His

own body on the tree, that we, being dead to sins, should live unto righteousness; by whose stripes ye were healed. For ye were as sheep going astray, but are now returned unto the Shepherd and Bishop of your souls" (1 Peter 2:24-25).

It might at first appear that Peter has digressed from his general theme in this passage. You may wonder how these doctrinal statements about our Lord's death relate to the matter of Christian submission to authority, even when we are mistreated. There is a clear connection, however, and it can be seen when we keep in mind the emphasis the New Testament writers place upon the power of an active faith. The apostle affirms these theological truths about the penal, subsitutionary aspect of Christ's death because belief in them becomes a dynamic in our lives, enabling us to do things we never could accomplish in our own strength. As we think with Peter about our Saviour's death on Calvary, therefore, we will find in it all the motivation needed to suffer in a Christlike manner.

First, we must take to our hearts the fact that Jesus *took the curse of our sin upon Himself.* Peter says that He "bore our sins in His own body on the tree." Those to whom Peter wrote would catch the significance of the expression "on the tree." In Old Testament times, the most shameful and ignominious thing that could happen to a person would be for him either to be killed by hanging or to have his body suspended from a tree after death (see Deut. 21:22-23).

When you and I reflect upon our Saviour's shameful death on Calvary's tree for our sins, we should be overwhelmed with gratitude. If He was willing to do so much for us, why shouldn't we be willing to suffer patiently for His sake?

Second, the apostle indicates that we must appropriate to ourselves the truth that Jesus died *to separate us from our sins:* "that we, being dead to sins should live unto righteousness." Here we are presented with the wonderful doctrine of our standing in Christ. The words "being dead" are a translation of the term used in classical Greek to describe the departed, the people who had died. Think of it! We bear the same relationship to our sins as the dead do to the world they left—none at all. God sees us, not as sinners, but as already "seated in heavenly places in Christ."

As we understand and apply this truth to our lives, we'll change in our attitude toward those who wrong us. Hating one's enemies and retaliating bitterly when wronged may be perfectly normal for sinners, but we must always remember that Jesus died on the cross "that we, being dead to sins, should live unto righteousness."

Paul expressed the same truth when he said, "Likewise, reckon ye also yourselves to be dead indeed unto sin, but alive unto God through Jesus Christ, our Lord" (Rom. 6:11). Putting this into practice is an exercise of faith—first, in taking to heart the truth that the death of Jesus Christ has brought us into a new standing before God as separated from our sins, and second, in deriving from it the dynamic for suffering wrong triumphantly.

The third aspect of Calvary we must appropriate to our lives is that Christ's death has brought us spiritual healing. The apostle declares this truth by citing Isaiah's declaration: "By whose stripes ye are healed" (53:5). As Peter reflects upon the scourging of Jesus, he sees it as bringing restoration from our spiritual sickness.

You see, mankind as a whole is selfish, cruel,

greedy, and immoral, and these are all symptoms of man's basic malady—his sinful nature. He suffers a deadly spiritual disease. Isaiah declared, "From the sole of the foot even unto the head there is no soundness in it, but wounds, and bruises, and putrefying sores. They have not been closed, neither bound up, neither mollified with ointment" (Isa. 1:6). As believers in Christ, our Lord's death has procured for us spiritual healing. This is yet another reason we need not despair when called upon to submit to wrongs in a truly Christlike manner.

The fourth benefit of Christ's death we must appropriate by faith is that it has brought us to God. No longer need we wander aimlessly, without direction or goal. This gives us yet another reason for suffering graciously. The apostle says, "For ye were as sheep going astray, but are now returned unto the Shepherd and Bishop of your souls" (1 Peter 2:25). As Shepherd, the Lord Jesus gives us guidance and protection, leading us safely to our home in glory. As Bishop, He oversees our lives, and gives us all the help we need to follow His example in patient suffering.

Summary

Peter has given us good news regarding our relationship to authorities—even in bad times of persecution and mistreatment. Let us review his message. He says first that God expects every Christian to be a good citizen. We are to submit to all who have positions of authority, even when we don't agree with them, even when we think their demands are unfair. This we are to do "for the Lord's sake."

We are to disobey human rulers only when compliance with their demands would mean breaking God's commands. We have a dual citizenship: we

live on earth but are citizens of heaven. Peter therefore calls upon us to adopt a proper submission to
human authority, a love for our brethren in Christ,
and a fear of God. We will thus "put to silence the
ignorance of foolish men."

How can we obey these high requirements? By
looking to Jesus. He set the perfect example for
us in suffering blamelessly, graciously, and trustfully. And, by faith we must weave into the fabric
of our lives the full truth of Calvary. Because Jesus
endured the curse of God's wrath against our sin,
died to give us a completely new standing, provided
healing for our spiritual disease, and brought us to
God, we can be different. By appropriating these
glorious truths, we can "take it patiently" when we
are wronged by the enemies of Christ.

6

You Can "I Do" Even If He Doesn't

(1 Peter 3:1-7)

Marriage as an institution is in deep trouble today. The divorce rate has increased to appalling proportions—and that's only half the story. Many husbands and wives, though continuing to live together, are desperately unhappy. They avoid seeking a divorce "for the sake of the children," or because they want to keep from disappointing parents or friends.

Such couples endure life under the same roof, perhaps refrain from unfaithfulness, and "keep up appearances." Meanwhile tension, hostility, and strife fester beneath the surface.

Many couples regularly consult marriage counselors, psychiatrists, or ministers, hoping to find some formula to restore marital bliss. But the road back to romance and tender feelings of mutual love is not easy, and few negotiate it successfully. In fact, it's almost impossible to repair a broken marriage relationship without the help of God.

Sad to say, these symptoms of unhappy marriage exist in many homes where husbands and wives are Christians. This displeases the Lord, and is totally unnecessary. You see, when both husband and wife are walking in fellowship with Jesus Christ, their marital relationship can be filled with love and real happiness. The Bible gives them all the instruction they need to live happily together, and the indwelling Holy Spirit Himself enables believers to obey God's will.

Included in Peter's letter to the believers in Asia Minor is a passage dealing with the marriage relationship. Significantly, the people he was addressing were facing many of the same problems confronting our own society. Infidelity was perhaps more commonplace than today, and the divorce rate was equally as high. Families were living under great pressures just as we are.

In addition, the church was undergoing persecution. Under such conditions, men lose their jobs, financial stresses occur, and ordinary problems seem to intensify. Then, too, many women who had become Christians were striving to maintain a successful relationship with unsaved husbands while continuing to be faithful to the Lord. Sometimes this was extremely difficult, especially when the man was antagonistic to the Gospel.

As we read 1 Peter 3:1-7, therefore, we find some biblical principles about marriage that apply to every age and society. Peter begins by addressing the wives, giving three specific qualities they ought to manifest; and then speaks to the husbands, telling them how they can properly fulfill their obligations.

Qualities of a Christian Wife

The apostle first instructs Christian wives to set as their goals the development of (1) proper submission, (2) God-fearing purity, and (3) beauty of spirit.

Proper Submission

The first virtue of the Christian wife is submission to her husband. Peter writes, "In the same manner, ye wives, be in subjection to your own husbands" (1 Peter 3:1). The principle laid down here is simply that the husband is to be recognized as the head of the home. It's the only way for a family to be united and happy.

Just as a team needs a head coach, and a business needs a director, president, or supervisor, so the home needs someone to be in charge. Peter says it should be the man. The wife might be more intelligent, have a more vibrant personality, or even hold a better job; yet in the home she must acknowledge the headship of her husband. This is God's will—and it works! A man who may not have great abilities can still be an effective husband and father if he depends upon the Lord and is led by the Holy Spirit.

The wife should be submissive even when the husband is an unbeliever. Her mate may stubbornly oppose the Gospel, but the Christian wife is to submit to his leadership. Peter writes, "In the same manner, ye wives, be in subjection to your own husbands that, if any obey not the Word, they also may without the Word be won by the behavior of the wives" (1 Peter 3:1).

The Greek verb rendered "obey not" is *apeithein,* a strong term which means "obstinately refuse to be persuaded." The husband may show some hostility or even become violently angry when his Christian wife talks about the Lord, but she should still be submissive to his leadership. She must not badger or harass him. She shouldn't quote Scripture to him all the time, nor harp at his every fault. Neither is she to neglect her obligations as wife, mother, and homemaker. Rather, she should be as winsome and lovable as she can.

When a man comes home from work and finds his wife cheerful and friendly, the home neat and tidy, and a meal tasty and well-prepared, and when he sees a beautiful spirit of Christlike submission in his mate, he may fall in love with her all over again. He will know that her faith is genuine and strong, and he may even offer to go to church with her. If the Christian woman heeds these suggestions, her husband could be "won by the behavior" of the wife. What happiness this would bring them both!

God-fearing Purity

The second quality a Christian wife should cultivate is a purity motivated by her deep reverence for God. Peter writes, "While they [the husbands] behold your chaste conduct coupled with fear" (1 Peter 3:2).

A member of the Radio Bible Class staff talked with an unsaved man who had been deeply impressed by his wife's loyalty and faithfulness since she had become a Christian. He said, "I know I'm not everything I ought to be, and I find myself thinking I don't deserve the kind of woman she is. I sure appreciate the fact that when my job takes me away for a few days, I know my wife is praying for me, and that her love for God and for me will keep her true. Her faith has really made her a good woman!" No wonder this man eventually came to know the Lord as his personal Saviour!

Spiritual Beauty

The third quality of a Christian wife is beauty springing from the heart. Peter declares, "Whose adorning, let it not be that outward adorning of braiding the hair, and of wearing of gold, or of putting on of apparel, but let it be the hidden man of the heart in that which is not corruptible, even the ornament of a meek and quiet spirit, which is in the sight of God of great price" (1 Peter 3:3-4).

The godly wife puts far more emphasis on her attitude and conduct than on her clothing or hair-styles. Now, let's not go to extremes and say that Peter is telling Christian women not to fix their hair or wear jewelry! No indeed! Remember, he also mentions the "putting on of apparel" in the same sentence, and he certainly isn't forbidding the wear-ing of clothing. Instead, he is telling the believing woman that the spiritual beauty she reflects because the Holy Spirit indwells her is far more important than the latest hairstyle or the newest high-fashion clothing. The beauty that is most significant comes from within, and shines outward like light through stained glass windows.

Peter uses two adjectives to describe the spiritual beauty that should mark every woman of God. He says she should have a "meek and quiet spirit."

The Christian wife is to be *meek*. This is the same Greek word that sometimes appears in the Gospels to describe the Lord Jesus. In Matthew 21:5, for example, we read, "Behold, thy King cometh unto thee, *meek*, and sitting upon an ass, and a colt, the foal of an ass." By riding into Jerusalem on a donkey instead of a beautiful battle stallion, our Lord ex-emplified gentleness, humility, and self-effacement.

I realize that Christian wives may at times find this exhortation to meekness a little difficult to ac-cept. It's not easy to be gentle when your husband continually drops his shirts, coats, ties, and shoes all over the house. It's hard to be meek when he criti-cizes your cooking or expects you to wait on him hand-and-foot while he loses himself in watching two consecutive football games on television. You'd like to yell at him, or hit him over the head with something.

You can let him know you're aggravated about his sloppy habits. You can even call his unfair demands to his attention. But be sure you do it with gentleness and meekness. He'll be more inclined to accept it graciously, admit that he's been thoughtless, and try to change his behavior.

Above all, don't fall into the habit of nagging or complaining. If you pester him all the time, hoping to make him uncomfortable until he does things your way, you may end up losing more than you gain. The two of you may get into big arguments, or he may start spending less time at home just to get away from the constant hassle. How sad it would be if he preferred the quiet of his office to the uproar of home!

Not only is the Christian wife to be meek, she is also to possess a "quiet spirit." The Greek word for "quiet" here is *hēsuchios,* and means "calm" or "tranquil." In her actions and reactions toward her husband, the children, and all of life in general, a woman is to avoid becoming anxious, nervous, and upset. She should continually remind herself that God is in control of the universe, and that He will not allow anything to come into her life except what is ultimately good for her and her family.

A woman must guard against going into an emotional seizure every time she encounters a mishap or thinks she has been wronged. After all, a burned roast is not the end of the world! A woman who is always in a tizzy about one thing or another doesn't make a home a very pleasant place to live. Nor does she show much evidence that she really believes God's Word, and walks by faith in His strength and grace.

In this regard, the apostle, speaking about certain godly women of the Old Testament, singles out Abraham's wife Sarah for specific mention. "For after this manner in the old time the holy women also, who trusted in God, adorned themselves, being in subjection unto their own husbands, even as Sarah obeyed Abraham, calling him lord; whose daughters ye are, as long as ye do well, and are not afraid with any terror" (1 Peter 3:5-6).

These women had such strong, abiding faith in God that Peter could call them "holy." Wives today, following their example, have no excuse for being rebellious or complaining. Sarah and her companions trusted God, and that was their secret. Every Christian woman by daily prayer, Bible reading, meditation, and practical obedience to the Scriptures, can in time develop a "meek and quiet spirit."

Qualities of the Christian Husband

I can well imagine what was going on in the church of Asia Minor while Peter's admonitions to the women were being read. No doubt some husbands were chuckling, and others were nudging their wives and saying, "See, I told you so!" But then it was time for the women to watch the men squirm, for the apostle shifts his attention to Christian husbands. "In like manner, ye husbands, dwell with them according to knowledge, giving honor unto the wife, as unto the weaker vessel, and as being heirs together of the grace of life, that your prayers be not hindered" (1 Peter 3:7). Three qualities, suggested by this passage, should be part of every Christian husband's relationship with his wife. He should develop (1) considerate understanding, (2) unselfish chivalry, and (3) spiritual awareness.

Considerate Understanding

First, the husband should be thoughtful of his wife and concerned about her feelings. Peter tells husbands to "dwell with them according to knowledge." A Christian husband must recognize the delicate nature of women. In many ways they are more sensitive than men. An unkind word, a thoughtless remark, the failure to remember an anniversary, or a complaint about a carefully prepared meal can hurt a woman deeply. If she is spiritually mature, she will most likely be able to keep her feelings under control, but the hurt will be there just the same.

Husband, you have a solemn obligation to understand your wife. Recognize the things that upset her, and avoid them. Think twice before making an angry or critical remark. Try to do what pleases her. Put into practice the admonition of Scripture, "Husbands, love your wives, even as Christ also loved the church, and gave Himself for it" (Eph. 5:25).

Usually a Christian husband doesn't intend to be cruel, but he can easily hurt his mate by sheer thoughtlessness or insensitivity. Remember and obey Peter's admonition, "In like manner, ye husbands, dwell with them according to knowledge." Provide loving leadership in your home, and be very careful about the feelings of your wife.

Unselfish Chivalry

The second characteristic of Christian husbands is a respect for the frailty of womanhood, "giving honor unto the wife, as unto the weaker vessel" (1 Peter 3:7). In New Testament times, the clay pots in common use were fragile, and some of them would crack or develop thin spots. These had to be handled with extreme care or they would break. This is exactly how the Christian husband should treat his wife—with tenderness and utmost consideration as the "weaker vessel." Though women's lib groups may not like to agree, it is a fact that members of the fair sex, because of their child-bearing capability, do undergo physical and emotional experiences that men do not have. Furthermore, their bodies are not as large and muscular. They just aren't as tough or strong, and are to be treated accordingly.

Peter's call for unselfish chivalry illustrates how the teaching of the New Testament has raised the status of women in Christian cultures. In the East it is common to see a man riding a donkey while the woman trudges alongside, carrying a burden on her head. In almost every part of the world where the Gospel has not been preached, women have always done the hard work while enjoying few rights and privileges.

I'm sure most of us are glad that the New Testament introduces true chivalry into the relationship between men and women. That's why a man, even though well-dressed, will stop to help a lady whose car is stranded along the highway with a flat tire. A husband instinctively reaches for a heavy door and opens it for his wife. It's not that she is too weak to do it, but it's easier for him. It also gives him a sense of satisfaction and self-worth. Besides, it helps her to realize that he loves her—and that's important!

We regret that some advocates of women's rights are busy tearing down these beautiful courtesies. Every Christian husband should continue "giving honor unto the wife, as unto the weaker vessel."

Spiritual Awareness

The third quality the Christian husband should cultivate is the spiritual oneness he and his wife enjoy as believers in the Lord Jesus. What a privilege to share the delights of your faith in Christ with the one you love most "as being heirs *together* of the grace of life" (1 Peter 3:7).

When both husband and wife are believers in Jesus, they share the joy of having been saved by the same grace and destined to the same heaven. A husband who acknowledges this will enjoy devotional times with his wife. He will listen to her as she tells of her experiences with the Lord. He will place great value upon her prayers as being just as important as his own. And he'll talk with her about their mutual problems, consider her opinions worth listening to, and show her in every way possible that he is glad they are "heirs together of the grace of life."

The spiritually minded husband is also aware that if he does not obey the admonitions of Scripture, he won't be able to pray effectively. The text says: "That your prayers be not hindered" (1 Peter 3:7). A lack of respect for his wife will put a barrier between a man and God. Someone has said, "The sighs of the injured wife come between the husband's prayers and God's hearing." By contrast, God answers the petitions of obedient Christians. There's no greater incentive for heeding Peter's exhortation.

Conclusion
God has given to Christian husbands the obligation to exercise leadership in the home, and this is to be done in a loving and considerate manner. The Lord also commands that you treat your wife as your spiritual equal. So, study the Bible together, pray with one another, and share in the God-given responsibilities of the home.

Christian wife, God has called upon you to be

submissive to your husband's direction, to be pure, and to reflect spiritual beauty through a meek and quiet spirit.

If you've entered a season of bad times in your marriage, or even if all is going well, take this good news from Peter seriously. When you do, you will find joy, peace, and beauty in living with your life partner. Your home will become more like heaven than any other place on earth. It will be a peaceful haven from the storms of life, a temple where God is worshiped, and a school where great spiritual truths are learned and lived. And, it will shine out to the world as a witness to the love of Christ.

7

Generally Weak Sunday Specials

(1 Peter 3:8-12)

The pastor of a Bible-preaching church, concerned that his congregation had failed to make an impact upon their small community, met with his deacons to discuss the problem.

One of the men hit the nail on the head when he said, "The trouble is with us! As Christians, our lives are fragmented. We tithe, attend church regularly, and spend time serving the Lord, but large areas of our lives are completely untouched by our faith.

"We abstain from certain practices we call 'worldly,' but otherwise our conduct is pretty much like that of the non-Christians around us. We complain, we look out for 'number one,' we become impatient when we drive; and, to be honest about it, we do a lot of things inconsistent with our faith."

He then concluded, "I guess *we lack integrity.* We just aren't as real as we ought to be."

This deacon had made a wise observation! He was describing not only the members of his church but many professing Christians. Our faith ought to encompass the whole person, but all too often we don't let it. Instead of honoring and serving Christ in every aspect of life, we are just "Sunday Christians."

A strong appeal for spiritual integrity may be found in 1 Peter 3:8-12, where five characteristics of the total Christian are set forth. They are: (1) unity of mind, (2) love for one another, (3) humility of spirit, (4) a forgiving disposition, and (5) a godly attitude toward all of life. Admittedly, these do not make up the entire scope of a believer's responsibility, but each is an absolute essential if we are to please God and be good witnesses for Christ.

Unity of Mind

First of all, believers in Christ are to be bound together by a singleness of heart and purpose. We should have a common concern for the souls of men and a common longing for God's glory as we work for the Lord. The Apostle Peter writes, "Finally, be ye all of one mind" (1 Peter 3:8). The Greek word he used for "one mind" is *homophrōn,* a compound of *homos,* which means "one and the same," and *phrēn,* which means "mind" or "disposition." We are to be one in aim and purpose as we witness to an unhappy and divided society.

This command for unity has been misinterpreted by a number of religious leaders as a plea for worldwide ecumenism. They take this passage as a denunciation of denominationalism. They say we can obey this command for unity by becoming indifferent to specific doctrines, and they press for a merging of all churches into one great united organization.

We strongly disagree with this idea! Bible-based convictions cannot be put off like a garment. In addition, when one is willing to consider as nonessential the doctrines of the virgin birth, the deity of

Christ, His substitutionary atonement, and His literal resurrection, he is compromising away the very heart of the Gospel.

We can better understand Peter's admonition to be "of one mind" if we remember that no denominational groups were in existence when he wrote. He was addressing members of small local churches, telling them to be united. When this advice is heeded, no one tries to gain a following for himself by coming up with some novel doctrine or by attacking the leaders of existing churches. If we do not agree with the teaching of someone who loves the Lord just as we do, we must not exaggerate our differences or make subtle accusations. Instead, we ought to meet with that person and discuss the problem in a spirit of love. We will often find it to be a matter of emphasis only, and both of us will learn from the discussion.

Even if two sincere Christians are unable to concur in their interpretation of some passage of the Bible, they can still maintain a oneness of spirit in Christ. They should teach the truth as they see it, and refrain from bitter attacks on one another. Those who agree on the fundamental doctrines can rejoice in their shared salvation despite minor areas of disagreement. The differences may be such that they cannot both affiliate with the same denomination, but they can still love one another in Christ and pray for their mutual welfare.

The founder of Methodism, John Wesley, set a good example. His preaching ministry began at the urging of his good friend George Whitefield. As time went on and the Methodist doctrine developed, however, the two men disagreed. Whitefield leaned more heavily toward Calvinism than his younger friend, and they parted company.

When Whitefield went to be with the Lord, Wesley attended a memorial service in his honor. Immediately after the meeting, a woman who agreed with Whitefield's views asked John Wesley, "Do you expect to see dear Dr. Whitefield in heaven?"

He replied, "No!"

"Ah!" said the woman, "I was afraid you would say that."

But Wesley quickly responded, "Do not misunderstand me. George Whitefield will be so near the throne of God that men like me will never even get a glimpse of him!"

Though differing in doctrine, Wesley did not lose the sense of oneness in Christ with his mentor and friend, and showed him honor and respect as a true brother in the Lord.

Love for One Another

The second characteristic of the total Christian is a compassionate, tender love for all men. Peter writes, "Having compassion one of another, love as brethren, be pitiful" (1 Peter 3:8). The Greek word translated "having compassion" is *sumpatheis,* and means "to feel with" or "to sympathize." Interestingly, this is the only place the word appears in the New Testament. A related term occurs in Hebrews 4:15, however, where we are assured that the exalted Christ as our Great High Priest can be "touched with the feeling of our infirmities."

When we use this word today, we think of sympathizing with someone who has experienced misfortune or sorrow. But in Peter's day the term also referred to sharing in the joy or happiness of another person. The command, therefore, is for us to join with others both in feelings of delight and of sadness. The Apostle Paul gave a similar instruction when he wrote, "Rejoice with them that do rejoice, and weep with them that weep" (Rom. 12:15).

This is good, practical advice! In effect, we're told to get out of the shell of our selfish little world and take a genuine interest in other people. Suppose you win a victory or achieve an important milestone. A brother or sister in Christ gives you a pat on the back and says, "Nice going! I'm happy for you!" How that would increase your joy! And, when you suffer loss or bereavement, how comforting it is to have a close friend at your side. An understanding squeeze of the arm, a card of sympathy, or a quiet "I'm praying for you" can mean so much in a difficult time. If we want others to share our joys and sorrows, let's also share theirs.

The apostle further commands us to "love as brethren," using the Greek word *philadelphoi*. Philadelphia, the "city of brotherly love," derived its name from this term. We ought to treat other Christians as members with us in God's family. All believers are brothers and sisters in Christ, and we are to demonstrate our true fondness for them.

As Peter wrote these words, he may have been thinking of the instructions Jesus gave His disciples on the night before His crucifixion. Our Lord said, "A new commandment I give unto you, that ye love one another; as I have loved you, that ye also love one another. By this shall all men know that ye are My disciples, if ye have love one to another" (John 13:34-35).

The Lord Jesus and His disciples consistently taught believers to love one another. In his first epistle, John emphasized the importance of brotherly love when he wrote, "We know that we have passed from death unto life, because we love the brethren. He that loveth not his brother abideth in death. Whosoever hateth his brother is a murderer; and ye know that no murderer hath eternal life abiding in him" (1 John 3:14-15).

We expect brothers and sisters in a family to manifest a special love for one another, and this at times leads to tremendous sacrifice. The same should be true within the family of God.

Another exhortation from Peter relating to our love for others is "be pitiful." This word refers to a deep inner feeling, a clutching at the inside. The term was also used by Paul: "And be ye kind one to another, *tenderhearted,* forgiving one another, even as God, for Christ's sake, hath forgiven you" (Eph. 4:32). The Gospel writers used the verb form of this word 12 times to describe Jesus' response to suffering, grief, and the heartache caused by sin. Our Lord was always sensitive to the burdens of others. And we ought to pray daily that God will make us tenderhearted and keep us that way.

This is in contrast to our society which has become calloused to human suffering and grief. Through the news media, especially television, we are confronted by a vast amount of heartache and pain. We see pictures of people wounded in war, dying from starvation, or suffering the aftermath of devastating floods or tornadoes. We can grow hardened until we are completely unmoved by the pain and distress of our fellowmen.

Then, too, life is so filled with activity, and the stresses of our complex world are so great, that we tend to become engrossed with our own problems. We don't let the sadness of others penetrate the thick skin of our insensitivity. How important that we consciously try to enter into the feelings of others and make an effort to help in any way we can.

A Spirit That Is Humble

The third characteristic of the total Christian, found at the conclusion of 1 Peter 3:8, appears in the Authorized Version as "be courteous." A number of versions, however, use the words "be humble" or a similar phrase. Assuming this to be an acceptable rendering, we will consider *why* we should be humble, tell *how* we can give evidence of our humility, and then provide a simple test to show how well we're doing.

Why should we be humble? Because we are sinners, and because we are created beings totally dependent upon the Lord. If we truly engage in self-examination on the basis of God's Word, measuring ourselves by the standards of His holiness, we will recognize how sinful we really are. We may think we're pretty good when we compare ourselves with some people, but this quickly changes when we glimpse the perfect holiness of God. Not only will this reveal to us our sinfulness, but it will remind us that we as created beings have nothing that has not been given us by the Lord. We'll acknowledge that the very continuance of our earthly life is dependent upon God's activity, for "in Him we live and move and have our being."

How is our humility made known? In lowliness of mind in relation to our fellowmen. This rules out all boasting about our accomplishments, showing off, or putting down another to make ourselves look good. If we are humble, we will also be uncomplaining when things go wrong, for deep in our hearts we know we really deserve nothing good. When we acknowledge the marvel of God's grace toward us, we will accept whatever comes from Him—even the difficult and bitter—as part of His good plan. We won't feel that God owes us a good job, vigorous health, or earthly acclaim just because we are who we are.

To discover how you rate in the matter of humility, let me suggest a simple three-part test you might give yourself. Your response will reveal whether you have an inflated sense of self-esteem, or just how much genuine humility you really have.

First, there is the *precedence test*. Do you feel badly when others are honored, because they outshine you? Are you filled with envy or dominated by a competitive spirit as you relate with other people? If you dispute about who is the greatest as Jesus' disciples did, you have failed this part of the test.

Second, what about the *sincerity test?* All too often people say things about themselves to sound humble, when really they are not. A man once made the statement, "I thank God that whatever faults I may have, I'm not proud!"

Actually, this statement itself manifests pride. So we're not surprised at what happened when someone responded, "You shouldn't be. You have nothing to be proud of!"

At this the self-proclaimed humble man indignantly retorted, "I haven't? Well, I've got as much to be proud of as you have!"

Let me ask again, can you pass the sincerity test?

Third, submit to the *criticism test*. Do you react unfavorably when someone points out your shortcomings? If you're rebuked, do you become hostile and defensive? Do you try to justify yourself? Maybe you retaliate by finding fault with the people who criticize you. Unless you can accept criticism graciously and are willing to learn from those who point out your failings, you are not truly a humble person.

If you have given yourself a perfect score, you've failed the humility test! As long as we live upon this earth we'll be fighting the battle against pride. Nevertheless, a pattern of victory can be ours in Christ if we really want it.

A Willingness to Forgive

The fourth quality of the total Christian is a willingness to forgive. Peter said, "Not rendering evil for evil, or railing for railing, but on the contrary, blessing" (1 Peter 3:9). We dare not kid ourselves into thinking that we can be good Christians if we fail to forgive.

It wouldn't be so hard if we were obliged to forgive only our loved ones or people who think well of us. But the Lord Jesus made it plain that God expects far more than that. He said, "But I say unto you that hear, 'Love your enemies, do good to them who hate you, bless them that curse you, and pray for them who despitefully use you'" (Luke 6:27-28).

Our Saviour gave us the supreme example of forgiving people who wrong us when from the cross He prayed, "Father, forgive them; for they know not what they do" (Luke 23:34).

The importance of a forgiving spirit cannot be overemphasized. If we refuse to forgive others, we live in disobedience to the Lord. An unforgiving spirit disrupts our fellowship with God and destroys our joy. How incongruous that a Christian, who has experienced the Lord's forgiveness of a mountain of sin and guilt, could be unforgiving in his attitude toward those who have wronged him. An unforgiving Christian is bound to be a miserable Christian.

Refusal to forgive has resulted in broken homes, wayward children, blighted lives, and both physical and spiritual distress. Some time ago I heard about a couple who remarried after having been divorced for 25 years. Their home had been broken up because neither would forgive the other after a quarrel.

Both had remained unmarried through those years, but one of their sons had died and the other had disappeared. The reconciliation came when the woman heard that her former husband was in the hospital, and she went to visit him. Suddenly they realized how foolish they had been, forgave one another, were remarried, and are now living together. What a price this couple paid because of their unwillingness to forgive! For a quarter of a century they were estranged from each other and unable to enjoy real fellowship with the Lord or experience the fullness of salvation. Besides, who knows how much suffering they brought into the lives of their sons?

If you are unwilling to forgive because you nurse a feeling of hatred or smoldering anger in your heart, you are hurting yourself and others. You may bring deep depression on yourself, for psychiatrists tell us that one of the primary causes of this emotional malady is inner anger. You may also bring physical affliction upon yourself, for doctors have discovered that many people who complain of one ailment after another begin to recover when they learn to forgive others. Above all, a tremendous spiritual obstacle rises between you and God.

David Augsberger, in his book *70 x 7* (Moody Press, Chicago), tells of a Christian man whose wife had become an alcoholic. He couldn't understand why she drank so heavily until one day she told him that she had had an affair with his best friend some 10 years earlier. She said her feelings of guilt after that episode led her to the bottle.

Anger and resentment swept over the man when he heard her story, for she had brought him and their children so much pain by her drinking. It also hurt him deeply to know that his close friend had betrayed his trust. But while these feelings welled up within him, the Holy Spirit brought to his mind the words of Christ, "Forgive us our debts, as we forgive our debtors" (Matt. 6:12). He knew what God wanted him to do. Yet he refrained from extending to his wife the forgiveness she so needed.

The Spirit of God continued to work in the offended husband's life, and here is his account of what happened the next time he saw the friend who had brought so much sorrow into his life:

> Then, with a sob in my soul, my hand came out and gripped his. . . . And for the first time in my life I knew what it was to forgive. For the first time I felt the tremendous sense of freedom, of liberty, of lighter-than-air release as the unbearable weight of bitterness washed out of me. And I was free. Free to forgive. Free to live again!
>
> And that new freedom not only gave me the strength to go on; it gave me the resources to love my way through that barrier between my wife and me too. When I told her, I forgive you! I accept you just as I did that day we pledged to love and cherish until death; then healing began its slow change (p. 12).

Christian, God expects you to forgive others. Completely! Even when the wrong is intentional and cruel! Let the Lord's mercy toward you become the pattern of your attitude toward others.

A Godly Attitude Toward Life

The fifth quality of the spiritually mature believer

is a godly attitude toward all of life. This in turn brings real joy and lasting contentment. Drawing from Psalm 34, Peter wrote,

> For he that will love life, and see good days, let him refrain his tongue from evil, and his lips that they speak no guile; let him eschew [turn aside from] evil, and do good; let him seek peace, and pursue it. For the eyes of the Lord are over the righteous, and His ears are open unto their prayers; but the face of the Lord is against them that do evil (1 Peter 3:10-12).

The meaning is clear: if you would love life, then guard your tongue, turn away from evil, do good, and live at peace with your fellowmen. As you practice these principles day after day, you will find true satisfaction. This is what we mean when we speak of a godly attitude toward all of life.

Some people have the mistaken notion that God doesn't want His children to be happy here on earth. Because many believers refuse to participate in some of the pleasures the world offers, and because they have a well-defined concept of sin, others may think they are frustrated and miserable. How inaccurate! God wants *all* who truly believe in Jesus Christ to live with a happy, contented, and optimistic outlook. He desires that we "see good days." Therefore, it's not wrong for a believer to be glad he's alive and to enjoy the legitimate pleasures earth affords. But true satisfaction is possible only when he obeys God's commandments.

In this passage (1 Peter 3:10-12), four distinct steps are outlined. First, the Lord tells every believer to guard his speech. "Let him refrain his tongue from evil, and his lips that they speak no guile," forbids us to speak maliciously. We must never engage in deliberate deception, innuendo, or misleading statements.

Second, we are to eschew or "turn aside from" evil. Whenever we're confronted with circumstances or situations that would lead us into a dead-end street of sin and its consequences, we're to turn aside and go in the other direction. We're to choose another road, just as we would choose a different road if we knew the bridge was out on our original route. Much heartache and misery would be avoided if believers were to "make tracks" when tempted and to stay away from places where sin is readily accessible. When temptation rears its ugly head, turn aside!

Third, if we would enjoy life, we are to "do good." The best way to shun evil is to do the will of God. Christianity is not only negative, but positive. How many believers, content to avoid the "thou shalt nots," miss the blessing of the "thou shalts." Preoccupied with "not sinning," they fail to do anything positive. Let us follow the example of the Lord Jesus, who "did no sin," but who also went about "doing good."

Fourth, we are to "seek peace and pursue it." We do this by giving a soft answer when someone verbally attacks us, by forgiving those who wrong us, by avoiding needless quarrels, and by willingly taking the lowly place.

If you're a Christian, are you happy? Do you love life? Are you seeing good days? If not, perhaps you're letting Jesus Christ reign in only a few compartments of your life, when He expects you to give Him *all* of it. You can start by following the suggestions of this passage from 1 Peter.

God's children have always found peace and happiness in the pathway of obedience. An aged Scot on his deathbed displayed the victory that is possible for every believer. He was asked, "Have you received a glimpse of Christ now that you're going to be with Him?"

The godly saint replied, almost with indignation, "I'll ha' none o' your glimpses now I am dyin'—seein' that I've had a full look at Him these 40 years!"

Paul, locked in a dungeon awaiting execution, wrote triumphantly,

> "For I am now ready to be offered, and the time of my departure is at hand. I have fought a good fight, I have finished my course, I have kept the faith; henceforth there is laid up for me a crown of righteousness, which the Lord, the righteous Judge, shall give me at that day; and not to me only, but unto all them also that love His appearing" (2 Tim. 4:6-8).

When you can die like that, you've learned how to live! The world may look upon a person with wealth, fame, and health and say, "That's living!" But that person may be miserable. A person who really lives is the Christian who walks in obedience to God.

If you're not a Christian, think about your desperate condition. You are a sinner. You are going to die. The whole world is on its way to destruction. Everything looks hopeless. You are living in bad times. But Jesus Christ offers you forgiveness of sin, strength for life, and hope for the future. Believe on Him, and you will be saved; submit fully to Him, and you will experience the satisfaction enjoyed only by the total Christian—a whole person in a world that is falling apart.

8

Here's What the Doctrine Ordered

(1 Peter 3:13-22)

Occasionally we receive a letter at Radio Bible Class that says something like this: "Why do you keep talking about specific things like the deity of Christ, the accuracy of the Bible, and the blood atonement? I believe in God and live a good moral life. Isn't that enough?"

Whenever I read comments such as these, I'm saddened, for I realize that the writer has no grasp of the rich and wonderful truths which are such a transforming power in the life of well-taught believers. I reflect upon the comfort that comes to my own heart in times of anxiety or bereavement because I believe the specific teaching and promises of God's Word. It's wonderful to know that my salvation is through faith alone, and it gives me joy to know that the Bible is trustworthy and that it gives me the guidelines I need to please the Lord.

What we believe is of vital importance. Failure to pay careful attention to the great doctrines can lead to spiritual shallowness and even departure from the faith. This is illustrated in the history of the

Pietistic movement. Pietism was a reaction to dead orthodoxy, which emphasized certain dogmas but not the accompanying walk with Christ. It began well, but when the Pietists went to the other extreme of neglecting doctrine, they paved the way for the theological liberalism of Schleiermacher and others.

The believers in Asia Minor may have begun to wonder how important it was to insist upon some points of doctrine and practice. Nero was beginning to persecute believers. Roman emperors could be ruthless. If worse came to worst, would some compromise be permissible? What truths are absolutely essential? These were questions they well might have been asking. To give these believers instruction, strength, and reassurance, therefore, Peter reminded them of two specific truths they could rest on with full confidence: (1) God is Lord of all, and (2) Jesus Christ was victorious over sin and death. In our study of 1 Peter 3:13-22, we will examine these two great doctrines, and outline their practical value for every believer.

Jehovah Is Lord of All
Peter first sets forth the truth that Jehovah, the one true and living God proclaimed in the Old Testament Scriptures, is the mighty Sovereign who controls every detail of life. We read,

> And who is he that will harm you, if ye be followers of that which is good? But and if ye suffer for righteousness' sake, happy are ye; and be not afraid of their terror, neither be troubled, but sanctify the Lord God in your hearts, and be ready always to give an answer to every man that asketh you a reason of the hope that is in you, with meekness and fear,

> having a good conscience, that, whereas they
> speak evil of you, as of evildoers, they may be
> ashamed that falsely accuse your good man-
> ner of life in Christ. For it is better, if the will
> of God be so, that ye suffer for well-doing
> than for evil-doing (1 Peter 3:13-17).

Two statements in this passage give assurance to
the Christian that he is safe regardless of his situation. In verse 15 we read, "But sanctify the Lord
God in your hearts," and in verse 17, ". . . if the will
of God be so." Both are expressions of God's sovereignty over all creation and every circumstance.

In the earlier and more reliable Greek manu-
scripts, the sentence translated "But sanctify the
Lord God in your hearts" often appears as "But
sanctify *Christ as Lord* in your hearts." Assuming
this to be the preferred rendering, we have a powerful affirmation of the deity of Jesus Christ. This is
because the apostle is quoting from Isaiah 8, a
prophetic passage in which the word "Immanuel"
(God with us) occurs twice in the Hebrew text (see
Isa. 8:8, 10). Peter had already drawn from Isaiah
for his reference to the Lord Jesus as "a stone of
stumbling, and a rock of offense" (1 Peter 2:8; see
Isa. 8:14-15). Now he cites Isaiah further to identify
Jesus Christ with Jehovah. Isaiah had written,
"Neither fear ye their fear, nor be afraid. Sanctify
the Lord of hosts Himself, and let Him be your fear,
and let Him be your dread" (Isa. 8:12-13). Since
this is clearly a Messianic passage, and the "stone
of stumbling" and "rock of offense" have already
been declared by Peter as references to Christ, we
would have to identify Him with the "Jehovah
Sabaoth" (Lord of hosts) of Isaiah 8:13.

Isaiah had declared that we should not fear men
but reverence Jehovah, and Peter is expressing the

same truth. When threatened by hardship or persecution, we can rejoice that the Sovereign of the universe is the triune God of the Holy Scriptures. Our faith is not anchored in a man, nor in some vague, mystical kind of power, but in a personal, living God who came to be "God with us" in the Person of Jesus Christ.

Peter makes a second reference to God's sovereignty, declaring, "For it is better, *if the will of God be so*, that ye suffer for well-doing than for evil-doing" (1 Peter 3:17). The expression "if the will of God be so" in the Greek is strikingly relevant for today, for it reads, "If the will of God should will it." When you believe everything is under the control of God, even opposition and disaster, you can face the future with confidence and hope.

A Sure Confidence

The first benefit derived from the truth of God's sovereign control over all things is a confidence that nothing in the world can bring a believer in Christ ultimate harm. Peter says, "And who is he that will harm you, if ye be followers of that which is good? But and if ye suffer for righteousness' sake, happy are ye; and be not afraid of their terror, neither be troubled" (1 Peter 3:13-14).

Instead of cringing in fright in the presence of persecution and adversity, the Christian can be confident that the triune God—Father, Son, and Holy Spirit—is in charge of the universe, and that every circumstance is under His control. He knows that unpleasant experiences have been permitted by the Sovereign Lord to help him spiritually, to lift him up, and to make him a better person. We may lose our jobs and be hated, or even be imprisoned and threatened with death because of our loyalty to Jesus Christ, but as long as we remain faithful to

Him, no real damage can come to us. Even if we die for our faith, it is not a tragedy, for Jesus told His disciples, "Be not afraid of them that kill the body, and after that have no more that they can do" (Luke 12:4).

The more you apply to your heart the truth that God is the Master and Sustainer of the universe, the more assurance you will have. The degree to which you exercise faith will be the degree to which you will be free from fear.

A Hope-Filled Testimony

A second practical benefit of faith in the sovereignty of the triune God is that it makes the believer a glowing witness in every circumstance. It provides him with a logical reason for his optimistic view of the future. The apostle says, "Be ready always to give an answer to every man that asketh you a reason of the hope that is in you, with meekness and fear" (1 Peter 3:15). When a person experiences salvation, he radiates confidence and hope, and people notice the difference. He boldly witnesses for Christ in obedience to the Lord's command. And when questions arise or opposition comes, he has a reasonable basis for the difference in his life. He's a new man, born again by faith in the Son of God, and he's not afraid to tell about it.

Not everyone, of course, can present a lengthy and scholarly answer for "the hope that is in you." It stands to reason that a person highly trained in apologetics will be able to set forth far more profound and intricate arguments for the faith than the average layman. But no matter who you are, if you are a Christian, you are able to tell people simply and clearly what Jesus Christ means to you. You can share the peace He brought to your heart, and the way He has changed your life. A first-hand testimony, taken from your own experience and based upon Bible truth, makes a powerful impact on the unsaved. But you must be certain your witness centers upon Jesus Christ as God and Saviour, and what He can accomplish in the lives of all who believe in Him.

The apostle instructs us to present our testimonies "with meekness and fear." We are not to give the reason for our faith in an arrogant manner. You see, we're not Christians because we're more intelligent than other people, or because something about us is especially worthy of God's favor. We're in His family because He reached down to us in grace, showed us our sinfulness, pointed us to Jesus Christ, and enabled us to believe on Him. If we are at all sensitive to spiritual reality, we will never get over the wonder of the fact that God saved us, and our witness will be in "meekness and fear."

A Godly Walk

When one believes that Jehovah is Lord of all, he will be inclined to live in a godly manner. People who view life as a process of continual change with no purpose or goal, leaving the Bible and Jesus Christ out of the picture entirely, will often give in to evil practices just because they see no point in trying to be good. But when one believes that God created and sustains the whole universe, and that He has provided a way of salvation for sinners, he has good reason to obey.

Peter therefore connects his admonition to acknowledge Jehovah's sovereignty with a direct appeal for godly living. He writes, "Having a good conscience, that, whereas they speak evil of you, as of evildoers, they may be ashamed that falsely accuse your good manner of life in Christ. For it is better, if the will of God be so, that ye suffer for

well-doing than for evil-doing" (1 Peter 3:16-17).
When we meet criticism or unjust persecution with
a life that is above reproach, we will not be plagued
by guilt nor haunted by the memory of our failures.
Furthermore, the people who are wronging us will
be put to shame when they observe our gracious
and forgiving manner as followers of the Lord
Jesus.

Remember, the world can't refute the testimony
of a godly life. In fact, it's the strongest of all arguments that Christianity is true. Your conduct speaks
far more eloquently than your words. Someone has
said, "A saintly person is one whose life makes it
easier for others to trust in Christ." Though a non-
Christian can find ways to criticize almost everything you believe, and may be more clever than
you in a debate, he is bound to take notice when
confronted with your transformed life. Your inner
peace and abiding joy will be evident to the unsaved, and your unselfish, forgiving spirit will give
shining witness that the Gospel works.

Christ as Victor over Sin and Death

Having emphasized the absolute sovereignty of Jehovah—the triune God who has proven His love for
us—Peter turns to a second grand theme: the Lord
Jesus, as the God-man, conquered death and destroyed its consequences. His perfect life, death on
the cross, and resurrection from the grave were all
on our behalf, and should draw from us an unhesi-
tating willingness to follow Him in every circumstance of life. As we study 1 Peter 3:18-22, we will
first develop the theme, found by connecting verses
18 and 22, and then examine two brief digressions
which occur in the intervening verses.

As the "last Adam," the Lord Jesus stood in our

place, suffering and dying for us. Read carefully Peter's words: "For Christ also hath once suffered for sins, *the just for the unjust,* that He might bring us to God, being put to death in the flesh but made alive by the Spirit. . . . Who [Christ] is gone into heaven, and is on the right hand of God, angels and authorities and powers being made subject unto Him" (1 Peter 3:18, 22).

The Lord Jesus, as God the Son, left heaven's glory to enter our sin-darkened world. In His lifetime here on earth He "did no sin," meeting unfailingly every demand of God's intrinsic holiness. He submitted Himself to the terrible ugliness of man's evil, bearing unjustly the agonies of rejection, betrayal, mockery, and the most horrible of deaths —crucifixion. He did it for us in love, turning undeserved suffering into glorious victory over sin and death. And, Jesus is now "gone into heaven," continuing His ministry in the place of majesty and honor.

Jesus' followers, united with Him by faith, are assured that the same beautiful progression will take place in their lives. His conquest of sin and the grave is ours by our belief in Him. We can look forward to life eternal in heaven—finally free from evil and all its consequences. What a glorious day awaits us!

Before we investigate the practical implications of our Lord's victory over sin and death, however, we will digress to consider the meaning of verses 19-21. Two complex problems for biblical interpreters confront us in this passage. The first, centering upon the "spirits in prison" reference (v. 19), has long puzzled Bible scholars. We will present the four better known explanations. The second problem is the "saved by water" section (vv. 20-21).

The Spirits in Prison

Peter, speaking of Christ, writes, "By whom also He went and preached unto the spirits in prison, who at one time were disobedient . . . while the ark was preparing" (1 Peter 3:19-20). Just who were these spirits? Your answer determines your interpretation of this perplexing passage, and dictates the answer to a second question, "What message was preached?" The word "preached" means "to herald" or "to proclaim," and can refer either to communicating the Gospel or giving an announcement. Four main views are held regarding the identification of these "spirits in prison."

1. They were the souls of the people to whom Christ preached by the Holy Spirit through Noah during the 120 years the ark was being built. Many good scholars hold this view, but it is not without problems. The antithesis expressed in the words, "being put to death in the *flesh* but made alive by the *spirit*" (v. 18), some claim, would more naturally refer to our Lord's human body and spirit than to the Holy Spirit. Furthermore, they object, to apply the term "spirits" to people is questionable. The Bible sometimes speaks of human beings as "souls," and mentions "the spirits of just men made perfect" (Heb. 12:23), but the Word of God never calls human beings "spirits." This term seems to be reserved for supernatural and nonhuman beings.

2. The "spirits in prison" were the mongrel off-spring of a union between fallen angels (the "sons of God" of Genesis 6:1-2) and women. Those who take this position contend that when Jesus died, He descended immediately into hades and announced to these imprisoned spirits that He had paid the price for sin. Objections to this view are that the purpose for this declaration is not given, and that

one must accept the theory that fallen angels were actually able to live in the marriage relationship with human women and produce offspring.

3. These spirits were wicked angels of Noah's day who engaged in some kind of monstrous evil, but who probably did not actually marry women. The people who hold this view consider the "sons of God" of Genesis 6 to be fallen angels who entered into or possessed the bodies of violent men. These men in turn fathered children with even more lawless traits. The term *nephilim,* translated "giants" in Genesis 6:4, thus would denote men who "fall upon" or attack others rather than "fallen ones" or "giants."

Scholars who give this explanation of the "spirits in prison" see the sinning angels of Genesis as the same ones to whom Peter referred as "delivered . . . into chains of darkness" (2 Peter 2:4). They say the purpose of Christ's entrance into hades was to tell this special group of wicked angels that their doom was certain. He had paid the price for sin and would soon demonstrate that He was indeed their Master by rising from the dead. This interpretation is possible only for those who feel that the "sons of God" of Genesis 6 were fallen angels, and that they possessed men's bodies and personalities for the purpose of leading the human race away from God.

4. The "spirits in prison" are wicked beings and Old Testament believers. Those who hold this view say that Christ descended into hades between His death and resurrection to make an announcement to all wicked spirits, and to release the Old Testament saints being kept there in a special compartment. Paul declares that Jesus "descended first into the lower parts of the earth" and "led captivity captive" (Eph. 4:8-10). Some Bible scholars see a dual purpose for our Lord's descent into hades. They say

He first announced to fallen angels that He had conquered sin and paid its penalty. Then, contending that the believers of the ages before Calvary were not fully forgiven until Christ had presented His sacrifice, they maintain that He went to them immediately after His death to take them to heaven. This view can be held only if one is convinced that the "compartment" theory of hades is biblical, and that Old Testament saints were not permitted to enter heaven until Jesus had died on the cross.

An exact identification of the "spirits in prison" is not possible. Because a reference is made to Noah, however, very likely they are either supernatural spirit creatures connected with the terrible conditions that led to the deluge, or the people to whom Noah preached while preparing the ark.

The "Saved by Water" Section

We are now ready to consider the second difficult section of this passage of Scripture. Peter wrote,

> Who at one time were disobedient, when once the longsuffering of God waited in the days of Noah, while the ark was preparing, in which few, that is, eight souls, were saved by water; the like figure unto which even baptism doth also now save us (not the putting away of the filth of the flesh, but the answer of a good conscience toward God), by the resurrection of Jesus Christ (1 Peter 3:20-21).

The best way to approach these verses is to examine the thoughts one by one as Peter expressed them.

1. *Noah and his family were "saved by water."* A little reflection makes it immediately clear that the water would have destroyed Noah and his family, not saved them, if they had not been in the ark. The flood, which killed the rest of mankind,

became the intermediary means of deliverance when it lifted the ark. If it had not, of course, the ark and its inhabitants would have been submerged, as were all of the highest mountains and tallest buildings.

2. *This scene of safety in the midst of judgment is portrayed by baptism.* Peter wrote, "The like figure unto which even baptism doth also now save us" (1 Peter 3:21). The Greek term translated "figure" is *antitupon,* and our word "antitype" is a transliteration of it. The water of baptism, therefore, is an antitype of the water of the flood. It therefore "saves" us in the same way the deluge "saved" Noah and his family. The water, representing judgment and death, buoyed up the ark so that its occupants were not drowned. Similarly, when we enter the water of baptism, symbol of judgment and death, we declare that we have found deliverance from the divine wrath because we are safe in the Ark; that is, in Christ. In His death on the cross He bore God's judgment against sin, and by faith in Him we have been brought into safety. When a believer is baptized, he signifies that through union with Christ he is rescued from condemnation and death.

3. *The water of baptism is not a cleansing agent.* The verse says, "not the putting away of the filth of the flesh" (v. 21). Baptism, rather than being the agent for cleansing, is "the answer of a good conscience toward God." The Greek word translated "answer" is *eperōtēma,* which means "question," "appeal," or "pledge." The latter fits this passage best, for baptism is a declaration by the Christian of his intention to "walk in newness of life" (see Rom. 6:4). This pledge issues from his clear conscience as a forgiven sinner, freed from guilt through his "by-faith union" with Jesus Christ.

Christ's Victory Applied

Having looked at these two digressions, let us now consider the significance of Christ's victory over sin and death for us today. First, it means that, as the Apostle Paul said, "Sin shall not have dominion over you" (Rom. 6:14). Its stranglehold is broken by the Lord's sinless life and sacrificial death on our behalf. We need no longer live in frustration or defeat, for the power of His conquest is at our disposal.

Second, if the Lord does not return before our lifetime is over, we have the assurance of the resurrection of our bodies from the grave. The "sting of death" is gone, replaced by the promise of the eternal life that awaits us. How marvelous to know that death is not the end! Sin is overcome and death is conquered. As citizens of God's kingdom, we can know that the blessing of being forever with the Lord awaits us. Because of Jesus' finished work, nothing remains to keep us from our heavenly home.

Conclusion

Faith and life are intertwined, and should not be separated. *What you believe* is directly related to *how you live,* as we have seen in 1 Peter 3:13-22. In this passage Peter applied two great truths about Jesus Christ to everyday life, and they are of great practical value to all believers.

First he emphasized that Jehovah is Lord of all. This truth is both encouraging and reassuring to the Christian. When we realize that He brought this world into existence and rules it in His providential care, we become confident and bold to witness. We find the grace to live a godly life that even the enemies of Christ cannot ignore.

Second, we're both humbled and thrilled when we appropriate the truth that the Maker and Controller of heaven and earth became a human being to pay the penalty for our iniquities and gain the victory over sin and death. We can face hardship and endure suffering victoriously as we look forward to an eternity with God. Yes, all of life becomes meaningful when kept in focus by the truths of God's Word. The "bad times" of this earth are but temporary and insignificant when seen in the light of divine revelation.

9

How You Look Is What You See

(1 Peter 4:1-11)

A desperate young woman on the verge of suicide was led to Christ by a pastor friend of mine. Carolyn's Christian parents had died while she was very young, and her only sister had been killed in an automobile accident. She was lonely, rebellious, and afraid. Life just didn't make sense to her. She had thrown herself into a frantic round of wild parties, experimentation, and excitement in her pursuit of happiness. But now she had come to the end of her rope. The life of gaiety couldn't erase her memory of past tragedies, and she was afraid to think about the future. Death seemed the only way out.

Then someone invited Carolyn to church, and she heard the message of the Gospel. She responded to the invitation to receive Jesus Christ as her personal Saviour. As she arose from her knees, she cried out in joy, "Everything looks different now! I don't want to die anymore. I feel peace in my heart, and I'm ready to live again. Even the future looks bright!" She had experienced divine forgiveness and had been born again. Everything was changed, and she was seeing herself and the world through new eyes. She could look back to the past and recognize God's hand leading her to faith, and look forward with hope to a life of happiness and peace.

At conversion, every believer in Jesus Christ receives a new, accurate perspective of himself, God, and the world. Peter speaks of this clarity of vision (1 Peter 4:1-11), showing us first how to view the past correctly, and then helping us look to the future with confidence and hope.

The Backward Look

First, the apostle gives his readers a backward look. This glimpse of the past begins with a view of the sufferings of Christ on Calvary, and then reviews the sins of his readers prior to conversion. It is good for all of us to remember the price paid for our redemption and the depth of depravity from which we have been delivered.

The Suffering of Christ

Any backward look is incomplete if it does not include the agony Jesus endured when He went to the cross for our redemption. Peter sees Christ's suffering as a source of great comfort to believers and challenge for the trials they must endure. He writes, "Forasmuch, then, as Christ hath suffered for us in the flesh, *arm yourselves likewise with the same mind;* for he that hath suffered in the flesh hath ceased from sin, that he no longer should live the rest of his time in the flesh to the lusts of men but to the will of God" (1 Peter 4:1-2).

The exact meaning of these two verses has long been debated by Bible scholars. We will examine the three main interpretations.

1. *Death ends sinning.* Some exegetes place great

emphasis upon the fact that the apostle is writing to Christians who would undergo persecution. Pointing to the words "arm yourselves likewise with the same mind," they say he is telling them to remember the way Jesus suffered and to follow His example. They see the phrase "for he that *hath suffered in the flesh*" as referring to death, pointing out that Peter used similar words just previously to depict Christ's crucifixion (3:18).

These interpreters consider these two verses to be a parenthetical word of assurance to Christians that if they die for Christ, they will be delivered from this world of sin.

Now, we can't argue with the conclusion that if a person dies for Christ, he ceases from sin. Of course he does, for he's dead. Furthermore, we recognize that persecuted believers can find inspiration in meditating upon Jesus' suffering, and that this will lead them to a more godly life. But we aren't sure that this passage can be restricted to persecution conditions.

2. *Suffering promotes godliness.* The second explanation of 1 Peter 4:1-2 is that affliction leads to godliness. Alan M. Stibbs, quoting Archbishop Leighton, said, "Affliction sweetly and humbly carried doth purify and disengage the heart from sin; weans it from the world and the common ways of it." Those who hold this view maintain that Christ's example, along with the hatred of the world, leads to a heavenly mindedness which rejects sin and promotes holiness.

3. *Union with Christ.* Most of today's biblical scholars, however, hold a third view—that Peter here is talking about our mystical union with Christ through faith. They say that the words "ceased from sin" are too strong to describe the sanctifying in-

fluence of suffering. They look upon 1 Peter 4:1-2 as parallel to Paul's statement in Romans 6:11, "Likewise, reckon ye also yourselves to be dead indeed unto sin, but alive unto God through Jesus Christ, our Lord."

Those who hold this view maintain that Peter is teaching the truth of our oneness with Christ. By an exercise of faith, we are to identify ourselves so strongly with the Lord Jesus that we see Him as dying for us, and ourselves as dying with Him; Him rising again for us and ourselves rising with Him; Him ascending and reigning for us in heaven and ourselves as ascending and reigning with Him "in heavenly places in Christ Jesus" (Eph. 2:6).

Regardless of which interpretation we take, the application is the same: when we contemplate the sufferings of Christ, our lives are to change. Peter says, "That he *no longer* should live the rest of his time in the flesh to the lusts of men *but to the will of God*" (1 Peter 4:2).

Notice the contrast in the words "to the lusts of men" and "to the will of God." The term "lusts" is plural, suggesting that unsaved people are controlled by varied and changeable desires. They are tossed to and fro by the fluctuating attractions, attitudes, and fashions of the world. Turning from one fad to another, they never know what they are going to believe next week or next year. They just want to make certain they are "in" with whatever is popular at the moment.

In actuality, they are being manipulated by money-making interests which determine what kind of books will sell the best and what type of music will make the greatest number of dollars. They are being victimized by those who prey upon the natural desire to conform. Even the more stable and thoughtful people often find themselves vacillating, groping for an authoritative, coherent moral and spiritual basis upon which to build a world-and-life view. This is why religious quacks often gain a big following, and it explains the reason theological fads like the "God-is-dead" movement become popular overnight. But how quickly these are forgotten!

The Christian, believing in one God who is revealed in Jesus Christ and the Bible, does not flounder about in a search for reality. Having the truth, he lives "to the will of God," finding in Jesus Christ the provision for all his needs.

The Sins of the Past

As the believer looks back upon his own life in the light of Calvary, he sees that much of his conduct was inappropriate for a child of God. Peter says, "For the time past of our life may suffice us to have wrought the will of the Gentiles, when we walked in lasciviousness, lusts, excess of wine, revelings, carousings, and abominable idolatries, in which they think it strange that ye run not with them to the same profligacy, speaking evil of you" (1 Peter 4:3-4).

All who have received Christ must renounce their former sinful behavior. To underscore this, Peter lists six specific sins of the past—practices to be rejected as incompatible with the Christian faith: lasciviousness, lusts, excess of wine, revelings, carousings, and abominable idolatries.

Lasciviousness—The first mentioned "sin of the flesh" believers must set aside is lasciviousness. This is the translation of a Greek word which means "excesses" or "open outrages against decency." It refers to public obscenities.

Now, I don't have to give explicit illustrations to demonstrate how prevalent this sin is today. If you have taken a look at the display of magazines in your drugstore or the theater ads in your newspaper, you need no further proof that lasciviousness is a grave evil in our culture.

We're in a pornography explosion! Why, any child with a dollar can purchase printed material filled with explicit obscenity. Movies and paperbacks are trying to outdo one another in human degradation. To add to the tragedy, some of our most respected news magazines are making light of the depths to which our society has fallen, but it's no laughing matter!

Lasciviousness is a serious sin because it violates the law of a holy God. The Lord is outraged when He sees men and women flagrantly breaking His prohibitions. Scripture says, "The way of the wicked is an abomination unto the Lord" (Prov. 15:9). As Christians, we must hate pornography and all forms of obscenity because the lusts they create and the sins they produce are evil in the sight of God.

It is serious, too, because of what it does to people. Only God knows the sum total of human misery brought on by indulgence in these excesses. As followers of Christ, we must sound out an earnest and solemn warning to all who are caught up in this evil. It leads to disaster, and every Christian must completely avoid it in every form.

Lusts—The second sin mentioned by Peter as he reviews the characteristics of the old life is *lust*. While lasciviousness has reference to the open promotion of sensual misconduct, lust has to do with the inner cravings of men and women. Many people, having enough human decency to denounce hard-core pornography, group sex, and shameful perversions, will nevertheless practice a life of "doing what comes naturally." They give God little thought and reject the absolutes of right and wrong set forth in the Bible, preferring to live by their own standards.

Sad to say, some of today's psychologists and counselors declare that it is harmful to suppress our desires. They tell people, "If you really want to do something, go ahead and enjoy it. Don't let feelings of guilt spoil it for you."

How contrary to the teachings of Christ! The Bible repeatedly emphasizes the necessity for self-control. There should be an ocean of difference between the life of a person governed by his own carnal desires and that of the believer who seeks to do God's will.

Excess of wine and revelings—The third and fourth evils listed by Peter—"excess of wine" and "revelings"—go together. These terms have reference to drinking parties and orgies. A leading United States senator recently declared, "The greatest problem in this country is alcohol." Knowing that drink has ruined thousands of lives, broken multitudes of homes, and caused untold heartbreak, a child of God certainly will recognize himself as out of his element at a drinking party with all its attendant evils. Though he may have indulged in this kind of conduct before he received the Lord, he now sees it as totally incompatible with his Christian testimony. He's happy with life as it is, and doesn't need the euphoria produced by a few drinks. The language and behavior of the tavern have become disgusting to him. And he wishes to avoid becoming a stumbling block to someone else.

Carousings and abominable idolatries—The final two sins Peter mentions as part of the sinful life of the unsaved are "carousings" and "abominable idolatries." These have reference to the immorality involved in the pagan festivals of the day—the "Mardi Gras" mood of totally unrestrained behavior. The heathen feasts of New Testament times involved suggestive ritual, ceremonial prostitution, and wild fervor brought on both by drink and the general atmosphere. Peter's declaration that these activities have no place in the life of a believer echo the warning of Paul, "Ye cannot drink the cup of the Lord, and the cup of demons; ye cannot be partakers of the Lord's table, and of the table of demons" (1 Cor. 10:21).

In our day we do not encounter the same forms of paganism present in the first century, but "carousings" and "abominable idolatries" are often included in occult practices, Eastern mysticism, and the drug culture. These movements have led many young people into despair.

Barry McGuire, a member of the original cast of one of Broadway's most famous stage plays, recently made this discovery. He testifies that he was in the process of destroying his life with drugs and sinful living when through the witness of Christians and the reading of the New Testament he began to see his lost condition and his need of Jesus Christ as Saviour and Lord.

He did not yield immediately, however, and one night attended a wild party. Suddenly, right there in the midst of all the artificial gaiety, he began to weep. A buddy said, "Hey man, what's wrong?"

"We are," came the reply. "We're wrong. This is wrong. Everything—our whole life-style is wrong!" To the amazement of all who heard him, he then declared with conviction, "Jesus is the answer!"

A proper view of reality had cut through all the make-believe of his drug-ridden life. Since that night, he has moved on to a satisfying walk with

God. He boldly proclaims that now he is happy and has a real purpose in living.

Yes, when a person becomes a Christian, he looks back on his past and turns away from the sins that mark the life of the unbeliever. One can adopt an Eastern religion, transcendentalism, the techniques of encounter sessions, or mysticism without abandoning his immoral ways. But it's different when one believes on Jesus. A person who receives Christ as his Saviour will recognize that lasciviousness, lust, and excessive wine, revelings, carousings, and abominable idolatries are not in keeping with the will of God.

Looking to the Future

Because of this new perspective, the Christian both rejects the sins of his past and walks a new pathway of obedience to God. Directing our eyes to that which lies ahead, and to the solemnity of life itself, Peter writes, "But the end of all things is at hand" (1 Peter 4:7). We live in the very shadow of eternity. Each morning might begin our very last day on earth. We may die before evening, or Jesus could return for us. This clear, realistic view of the future led the apostle to issue four practical admonitions. He tells us to live soberly, prayerfully, lovingly, and faithfully as we prepare for eternity.

Sane and Levelheaded

The apostle's first exhortation is, "be ye, therefore, sober-minded." The Greek word translated "sober-minded" is *sōphronēsate,* and means "to be in one's right mind" or "to be in control of one's passions." It was the term used to describe the demoniac at Gadara after the Lord had cast the demons out of him (see Mark 5:15).

Christians are to maintain rational control at all

times, avoiding the extremes of wild excitement or morbid depression. We're to keep from the frenzied pace of those who think this life is all there is, and who try to "grab all the gusto they can get." Likewise, we are not to be paralyzed by the fear of death. Believing that Jesus paid the price for our sins and broke the power of death, we can be calm as we anticipate the glorious eternity that awaits us. With this accurate perspective of the future, we can keep our minds and emotions in balance, and therefore live sensibly.

Be Prayerful

Peter's second admonition to believers is, "Watch unto prayer." Recognizing the seriousness of life and the imminence of the Lord's return, we are to utilize the privilege of prayer. The Greek expression "watch unto prayer," literally translated, is "be serious unto prayer," indicating that it is solemn business and demands our full attention. We are not to become frivolous, selfish, or irresponsible in our praying, for prayer *does* make a difference.

As you approach the Throne of Grace, be thankful and offer the Lord your sincere praise. As you present your requests, place greater value on spiritual and eternal riches than upon the material and temporal. Learn to say, "Thy will be done." Remember, you maintain your fellowship with God through prayer. It's the lifeline through which you can keep fresh the awareness of His love and presence, and express your concern for others.

Be Fervent in Love

The apostle's next command is, "Have fervent love among yourselves; for love shall cover the multitude of sins" (1 Peter 4:8). The word "fervent" comes from the Greek term *ektenēs* which means "stretched out." This is descriptive of the taut muscles of an athlete or the neck of a horse as he strains to win a race. We are to have unselfish concern for others in such an intense way, stretching to the point of sacrificial giving of ourselves for their welfare.

This kind of love covers "the multitude of sins." Only the blood of Jesus Christ takes away sin; our love cannot do that. Therefore, this phrase must mean that one who loves fervently forgives the other person again and again and again—not just seven times, but seventy times seven (see Matt. 18:21-22).

Fervent love also leads to hospitality. Peter continues, "Use hospitality one to another without grudging" (1 Peter 4:9). In Bible days, traveling was difficult. Inns were few, and those that were available were usually dirty and expensive. Often they were centers of immorality. This meant that when Christians journeyed to a new area, it was a great relief to have fellow believers invite them to stay in their homes. Today, though conditions have changed considerably, we should manifest the same spirit of hospitality. Christian courtesy never goes out of style.

Be Diligent

Peter's final exhortation is for believers to be diligent in the use of their talents. He says, "As every man hath received the gift, even so minister the same one to another, as good stewards of the manifold grace of God. If any man speak, let him speak as the oracles of God; if any man minister, let him do it as of the ability which God giveth, that God in all things may be glorified through Jesus Christ, to whom be praise and dominion forever and ever. Amen" (1 Peter 4:10-11). Remember, we have been given certain gifts and must answer to God for how we use them. We do not live in isolation, but as members of the Christian community we are interdependent. Our duty is to help one another on our pilgrim pathway, using our gifts to minister to the needs of people.

Peter distinguishes between two types of ministry. First he mentions the spoken word, "If any man speak, let him speak as the oracles of God." We must be careful to declare God's Word accurately and with deep conviction, realizing that it comes from the Lord Himself. When we speak, it must be in keeping with the revelation of God's truth.

Second, the apostle emphasizes service, referring to deeds of practical kindness, mercy, and helpfulness. "If any man minister, let him do it as of the ability which God giveth." Whether we do custodial work, drive a church bus, work on a welcoming committee, go out calling, visit the sick and shut-ins, or take care of administrative details, we should do so with zeal and wholehearted devotion. When we do the work of God, we are building for eternity. Let us therefore keep ever before us the prospect of hearing Jesus say, "Well done, thou good and faithful servant."

Perhaps "bad times" have obscured your vision. Right and wrong seem so much alike, and you're not really sure it makes any difference anyway. You don't know what's best for you, and the future seems uncertain and scary.

Then let me urge you to adopt the "good news" of God's Word. It shows us that the way of the flesh—marked by the sins of lust, drunkenness, and reveling—leads to unhappiness and ends in eternal separation from God. It also reveals that the life of faith in God, trust, obedience, and service brings peace of heart, confidence, and an anticipation of future glory.

The good news is that you can be on the second pathway. If you're a Christian, totally renounce the old way of life and submit to God's will for your life.

If you're *not* a Christian, I would urge you to receive the Lord Jesus today. He came to earth to live a sinless life for you, and die on Calvary's cross for your sins. He arose from the grave to bring you victory over death. Right now He offers you the forgiveness of sin and hope of eternal life. Why not take advantage of His gift? Receive Him now as *your* personal Saviour.

10

This Trouble Is for Good

(1 Peter 4:12-19)

It isn't hard to live the Christian life successfully when all is going well. Most of us, blessed by a measure of prosperity and good health, encouraged by worship and fellowship, and secure in a country which grants us religious and personal freedom, find it relatively easy to maintain a degree of spiritual integrity.

But what about those times when things go wrong? What if financial ruin, poor health, or extreme sorrow and disappointments come? What if our religious freedom is taken away? What if we're openly opposed for our faith in Christ, and persecution and even death become real threats? These are good questions for us to think about, for we have no guarantee that our situation will always be untroubled. Furthermore, we know that in some parts of Africa, Asia, and Eastern Europe, believers right now are suffering and sometimes dying for their faith.

Yes, "bad times" are bound to confront every Christian. He'll experience disappointment, heartache, and loss. Even persecution or martyrdom cannot be ruled out as possibilities for some in the future. Yet, in 1 Peter 4:12-19, we find "good news" for all in difficult times. Anticipating the hardships the believers in Asia Minor would soon endure, Peter listed three attitudes of mind and heart which are to characterize believers whenever they are called upon to suffer for their faith. We will consider each of them carefully, applying them to our lives today.

Don't Be Surprised!

Peter begins by calling for Christians to maintain a realistic view of their relationship to this world system. We know that our home is in heaven. We're aliens and pilgrims here, traveling through hostile territory. We can't expect the Christian life always to be a sunlit, primrose pathway where we can skip blissfully on our way to eternity. Facing squarely our "sojourner" status, we're not to be surprised by adversity. "Beloved, think it not strange concerning the fiery trial which is to test you, as though some strange thing happened unto you" (1 Peter 4:12).

Even though we've been born again, we're still finite creatures in a fallen world. We need not be shocked or dismayed, therefore, when misfortune strikes. In fact, we should anticipate times of hardship, and mentally and spiritually prepare ourselves to meet them. When they occur, it doesn't mean God has forgotten us, or that He no longer loves us. This kind of reaction can only lead to spiritual paralysis and defeat. By realistically viewing ourselves in relation to the world, we won't be taken by surprise.

On occasion, the "fiery trial" may take the form of open persecution by the enemies of the Gospel.

No Christian, if he has read the New Testament and knows anything about church history, should be surprised if he encounters this himself.

The Book of Acts records the scourging and imprisonment of Peter and John, the stoning of Stephen, the execution of James, and organized opposition to all believers. Saul of Tarsus, who had himself persecuted the church until he met the Lord Jesus and became Paul the apostle, tells us that he was scourged with whips five times, beaten with rods on three occasions, stoned and left for dead once, and often imprisoned (see 2 Cor. 11:24-27).

From the infancy of the church in Jerusalem through its adolescence in the Roman Empire and Middle Ages, right down to the present, believers in Christ have known and lived with bitter hatred from godless men. But God's work has gone on. Though the wicked have mercilessly tortured followers of Jesus and have cruelly taken the lives of many, they have been unable to put an end to the witness of the Gospel.

As believers in Christ in the last quarter of the 20th century, we have no guarantee we will be kept from experiencing antagonistic and hostile action by the world. Atheistic communism still looms as a threat to all who are truly born again. And, in the free world, many current signs indicate a growing polarization of Christian and non-Christian factions. The rapid increase in the number of Christian day schools and general trends in government are evidences that this is occurring. Peter's words may take on additional meaning, therefore, as the century draws to a close.

The Lord has not promised us exemption from crushing disappointments, pain, bereavement, or persecution. Any one or all of them could come. If they do, don't be surprised or perplexed. Accept them as part of Christianity, and call upon God's strength to endure.

Rejoice!

After telling believers not to be surprised when the fiery trial comes, Peter makes the startling statement that they should actually rejoice! "Wait just a minute!" you say. "That's not realistic at all! I can see where I shouldn't be taken unawares when suffering comes, but this doesn't mean I have to be happy about it. After all, it's hard to endure persecution or affliction. What does Peter mean?"

The apostle presents us with two good reasons for rejoicing in suffering: (1) The degree to which we endure hardship submissively will be the measure of the glory we will receive in heaven. (2) Affliction becomes the means by which the reality of God's presence is manifested in and through us.

Riches in Glory

We can rejoice, first of all, because God has promised us eternal blessing to the degree that we must suffer. Peter says, "But rejoice, inasmuch as ye are partakers of Christ's sufferings, that, when His glory shall be revealed, ye may be glad also with exceeding joy" (1 Peter 4:13).

Peter instructs us to view our present trials from the perspective of eternity. When we walk with Jesus Christ, submitting to His plan and remaining faithful to Him, our suffering down here will result in additional delights in heaven. The word translated "inasmuch as" in this verse means "to the degree that" or "in the same measure that." The passage could therefore be rendered, "But rejoice to the degree that ye are partakers of Christ's sufferings." Thus we learn that our suffering on earth has a direct correlation with the riches we shall receive in heaven.

The story is told of an atheist whose pumpkin crop flourished while his Christian neighbor's froze. Taunting the believer, he asked, "Why did God let your pumpkins freeze? Mine are all right."

The reply came, "God is not raising pumpkins. He's raising men!"

How true! This believer understood the reason for suffering, and rejoiced in it.

Of course it isn't easy to rejoice when tragedy strikes. But whenever one rebels or gives in to despair, he robs himself of the fullness of blessing he could have. A middle-aged man and his wife lost a son and a daughter, both in their early 20s, in separate automobile accidents within the space of one year. Surges of bitterness and anger overwhelmed the father. He wondered why God had permitted this double tragedy in their family. For a few years he didn't go to church, not because of rebellion but as a result of his deep hurt and bewilderment. Today he has an excellent attitude, but sorrow and confusion temporarily brought havoc into his life. While we can sympathize with his reaction, we regret the years he lost because he did not follow Peter's admonition to rejoice.

The second reason for rejoicing is found in verse 14. Peter says, "If ye be reproached for the name of Christ, happy are ye; for the Spirit of glory and of God resteth upon you; on their part He is evil spoken of, but on your part He is glorified" (1 Peter 4:14).

When the apostle used the expression "Spirit of glory," he most likely was thinking of the *Shekinah* of the Old Testament. This was the pillar of cloud by day and fire by night through which God manifested His presence among the Israelites as they journeyed in the wilderness (see Ex. 33:9-10; 40:34-35). The people of Israel, seeing this cloud by day and fire by night, were assured that God was with them and was leading where He wanted them to go. Just as the *Shekinah* was a visible symbol to God's ancient people, so the reality of the Holy Spirit's presence in us should be a cause of rejoicing for believers today.

The glory of the indwelling Spirit ought to be seen by everyone with whom we come in contact. He shines forth brightly and unmistakably when we rejoice in the midst of affliction.

This happened in the life of Stephen, the young deacon who became the first martyr of the Christian church. Luke describes him as he stood before men determined to put him to death: "And all that sat in the council, looking steadfastly on him, saw his face as it had been the face of an angel" (Acts 6:15).

There shone from Stephen's countenance a brightness, a calmness, and a confidence that reflected the Holy Spirit's work in his life. He knew his death was imminent, but still he glowed with a radiance which could come only from God. A pagan or an unbeliever may face the end of his earthly life heroically, but only a Christian can die forgivingly. Many men may die bravely, but only a believer can die triumphantly.

Christian martyrs since the day of this stalwart young deacon have followed his courageous example. In my mind's eye I can see thousands of people gathered in a large arena, seated on stone tiers. They have come to watch athletes demonstrate their skills, but that is not the main attraction.

The great cry goes up, "The Christians to the lions!" A door opens, and a small band of men, women, and children walk slowly to the center of the stadium. Calmly, and without a trace of hatred or fear on their faces, they kneel together on the ground. They pray, and then rise from their knees to sing the hymn found in 2 Timothy 2:11-12.

> It is a faithful saying:
> If we be dead with Him,
> We shall also live with Him;
> If we are called to suffer,
> We shall also reign with Him;
> If we deny Him,
> He also will deny us.

Before the song is ended, the hungry lions, which have been starved for a week, are released from their cages, and in a few moments it is all over on earth for the Christians.

I say to myself, "Why did they die that way? Just a few grains of incense on a pagan altar, just a word of veneration for the image of the emperor, and they could have walked again under the light of the sun to the embrace of friends and relatives." But to take this way of escape from violent death was abhorrent to them, for they had experienced the reality of Jesus Christ and His salvation. They knew their bodies were the temples of the Holy Spirit, and in their dying they manifested His presence in the glow of faith that could be seen upon their faces.

On more than one occasion history records that the stalwart faith and vibrant testimony of Christian martyrs has resulted in the salvation of their executioners. The story is told of a certain legion of 100 Roman soldiers that had been drawn especially close together through their shared experiences in battle. Among them was a band of 40 Christians. The day came when the emperor called for a test of loyalty throughout the army. Every recruit was to pour out a libation before an image of the emperor. As these 40 men went forward one by one, each said, "I am a Christian," and refused to worship the idol. They were sentenced to death. Their commander, though heartsick because of the comradeship he felt for them, ordered the men out onto the ice to die of exposure. As they went, the little group chanted, "Forty wrestlers, wrestling for Thee, O Christ, claim for Thee the victory and from Thee the crown." Their leader waited all night by a large bonfire on shore, hoping the men would recant and come to offer worship. Finally, late in the night, one half-frozen man stumbled into the fire's glare and fell exhausted before the image. The other 39, however, stood firm, determined to die for Christ if need be.

So impressed by the devotion of these Christians was the commander that he threw aside his armor, sword, and shield, and ran out to join the dying men. Soon the chant again was heard echoing over the frozen wastes, "Forty wrestlers, wrestling for Thee, O Christ, claim for Thee the victory and from Thee the crown." Yes, it's just as Peter said, "If ye be reproached for the name of Christ, happy are ye; for the *Spirit of glory* . . . resteth upon you" (1 Peter 4:14).

We have been talking here about persecution, but the Holy Spirit's presence should be seen whenever we suffer, whatever the cause might be. And it *will* if we accept God's way without dismay, rejoice in the assurance that He is working out His loving purposes, and remember that the Spirit of God dwells within us.

Commit Yourself to God

The third admonition to believers going through "fiery trial" is that they humbly commit themselves to the Lord. "Wherefore, let them that suffer according to the will of God commit the keeping of their souls to Him in well-doing, as unto a faithful Creator" (1 Peter 4:19).

This calm repose in God certainly makes sense! After all, He brought us into existence. He made provision for our salvation in the person of His Son. And, He has given us His Word with all its wonderful promises. He changed our lives and gave us peace within our hearts. Isn't it logical, then, that we commit the keeping of our souls to Him in all of life's circumstances? The answer, of course, is a resounding "YES!"

Peter has been talking about suffering which comes "according to the will of God." But now he includes a warning: "Let none of you suffer as a murderer, or as a thief, or as an evildoer, or as a busybody in other men's matters" (1 Peter 4:15). There are times when a Christian brings difficulties upon himself. He may steal, break laws, speak against others, or even commit murder. If he is caught and punished, he is *not* to look upon this as persecution. Suffering the consequences of a lying tongue or a meddling manner is not partaking of the affliction of Christ, either. Every believer must so live that his suffering, when it comes, will be "as a Christian."

How do you react when trouble comes your way? What do you think would be your attitude if you were faced with terrible persecution or called to go through "fiery trials"? Don't make the mistake of shrugging off these questions as irrelevant, or evaluating Peter's exhortations as idealistic and impractical. Remember, he was not merely theorizing, for even as he wrote this first letter, he knew martyrdom awaited him. The Lord Jesus had told him that the day would come when men would bind him and take him away to his death (see John 21:18-19).

In his second letter, written about a year later, Peter spoke of his impending death, saying, "Knowing that shortly I must put off this my tabernacle, even as our Lord Jesus Christ hath shown me" (2 Peter 1:14). Yet in all of his writings, we do not find a single trace of fear or dismay.

You can be triumphant, as Peter was, if you follow his admonitions. First, don't be surprised when suffering comes, but view it as a privilege which leads to eternal glory and blessing, and rejoice in it. Face your situation squarely, realizing that the Holy Spirit dwells within you. Let Him fill you with such confidence that your life will reflect His presence. Third, commit yourself to the Lord completely, believing with all your heart that He will keep you safe for His eternal glory. You will be able to view the "bad times" in true perspective, and this in turn will bring honor and glory to God.

11

The Pastor Plan

(1 Peter 5:1-7)

As I go about preaching in different churches, I can often sense a particular atmosphere as soon as I walk on the platform. When I look out at the people, I sometimes see boredom and apathy. At other times joy and enthusiasm glow on their faces. This contrast is carried on through the whole service—in the way people sing, listen to the announcements, and respond to the sermon. When I leave some churches, I say to myself, "If I lived here, I'd love to be part of this assembly." On other occasions, however, I find myself wondering why anybody attends.

The first New Testament believers were exuberant when they gathered for their meetings. Luke, speaking of the people converted on the day of Pentecost, says that they, "continuing daily with one accord in the temple, and breaking bread from house to house, did eat their food with gladness and singleness of heart, praising God, and having favor with all the people" (Acts 2:46-47). One in spirit and purpose, they found delight in God and in one another. No wonder so many thousands became Christians during that first century!

Today, however, an outsider is likely to get an entirely different impression of the church. He may go to a service where everybody acts as if worship were a tiresome ritual. He may be disillusioned by reading newspaper accounts of strife and dissension within denominations. He may work alongside of Christians who talk about turmoil in their assemblies—trouble stemming from pastor-people problems, petty jealousies, or power struggles between members. As a result, this onlooker may decide that Christianity has nothing to offer him. He has enough problems already.

The failures and faults of organized religion have also made a negative impact on some Christians. They have come to the conclusion that they can grow better spiritually by leaving the church altogether and studying the Bible on their own or with a few friends. But this is a defeatist attitude, and is not right!

God established the church for our good. He has bestowed gifts upon its members and has set forth instructions regarding its organization and function. Therefore, we should be active participants. Paul says the ascended Christ gave apostles, prophets, evangelists, pastors and teachers to the church "for the perfecting of the saints for the work of the ministry for the edifying of the body of Christ" (Eph. 4:12). He also lists qualifications for men filling the offices of elder and deacon (see 1 Tim. 3). Such offices presuppose an organized church. The local church, therefore, has a central place in God's program, and we should work and pray that ours might be what He intends it to be. Yes, God's will is for churches to be happy, growing, and effective. And they *can* be, even in today's tumultuous world!

The fact is that many thriving churches can be found throughout the world. They are glowing testimonials of the wonderful blessings God gives a local assembly when its members are living in obedience to the Scriptures. Peter addresses both leaders and congregations (1 Peter 5:1-7), giving specific instructions to each and encouraging them with the wonderful promise of "a crown of glory" (v. 4).

Responsibilities of Elders

The apostle begins by speaking to the elders, identifying himself as one of them, and then telling them how the Lord expects them to live. "The elders who are among you I exhort, who am also an elder, and a witness of the sufferings of Christ, and also a partaker of the glory that shall be revealed: feed the flock of God which is among you, taking the oversight of it, not by constraint but willingly; not for filthy lucre but of a ready mind; neither as being lords over God's heritage, but being examples to the flock" (1 Peter 5:1-3).

Those whom Peter called "elders" were primarily the men holding official positions of leadership within the church, but the term may also have included all the older members of the congregation. We do know that in the New Testament the term *presbuteros,* translated "elder," usually denotes a leader. (In Judaism, this word referred to a ruler in the synagogue, and in some cases a member of the Sanhedrin—see Mark 8:31; Acts 4:5, 8; 6:12; 23:14. In the Greek world the word referred to men with civic or religious duties, such as a member of the ruling body of a city.) This term, with its rich background in both Jewish and Greek history, was chosen by the Holy Spirit to designate those who served as officials in the churches. Peter, who himself was an elder, exhorted men holding this position to shepherd the flock, willingly, joyfully, and humbly.

Shepherd the Flock

Peter's first admonition to elders is that they serve the people in their congregation like a shepherd cares for his sheep. We read, "Feed the flock of God which is among you" (1 Peter 5:2). The Greek verb translated "feed" is *poimanate*, the imperative form of the verb which means "to shepherd." The same root word, in its noun form, is translated "pastor." As shepherd, the elder will provide spiritual food for his people by teaching them the Bible. But that isn't all he does. He prays for every believer God has placed in his charge. He comforts them and watches over them to keep them from straying. He goes after those who have wandered away. And he guards his flock against wolves, the false teachers who would destroy his flock, and against Satan, the "roaring lion" who would devour them.

The emphasis upon the work of shepherding indicates the tremendous responsibility God gives the pastor of a local church. Being an undershepherd of God's flock is a noble trust, and no man should enter the ministry lightly. Everyone who holds this office must carefully weigh the words of Christ, "For unto whomsoever much is given, of him shall be much required; and to whom men have committed much, of him they will ask the more" (Luke 12:48).

The duties of the pastor are many and complex, and he must live in continual dependence upon the Lord. Praying, preparing sermons, counseling, comforting, rebuking, and sharing the joys and sorrows of others add up to a task for which no human being is capable apart from the enabling work of the Holy Spirit. But God has provided for the needs of every pastor He has called, and has laid out his responsibilities in exact detail. There is no excuse for being aimless or haphazard in doing the work of God.

Serve Willingly

Peter's second exhortation to elders is that they fulfill their office with a willing spirit. He says, "taking the oversight of it, not by constraint but willingly" (1 Peter 5:2).

No leader should perform his task reluctantly. A man who believes he is called into the ministry should not fulfill his responsibilities grudgingly, as if they were an unpleasant ordeal or just a job to get done. When he gets up to preach, it should be obvious to everyone that his whole heart is in his message, and that he is thrilled with the opportunity God has given him. When he makes his hospital calls, his delight in being the Lord's servant should be obvious to everyone. If I were bedridden, I wouldn't care to have a pastor call on me if I could tell that he didn't like doing it.

Peter says the shepherd should serve "not by constraint." The pastor should be so convinced he is doing God's will that he serves with joy. Admittedly, some aspects of the ministry are difficult. It isn't easy to rebuke someone who has done wrong, or bring the news of a death to a family. It's hard to minister to parents whose youngster has been killed in an auto accident or to parents whose children are in trouble. But if a man believes God has called him, he can't be happy doing anything else.

Serve Unselfishly

The third admonition to elders forbids selfishness

and calls for an enthusiastic attitude toward the task they have accepted. We read, "Not for filthy lucre but of a ready mind" (1 Peter 5:2). The term "filthy lucre" is not common in our vocabulary. It involves more than money, for it carries with it the idea of "fondness for dishonest gain." The godly pastor isn't in it for himself, but serves his people willingly and with enthusiasm. He eagerly and freely accepts his position. He loves his work of shepherding the flock, and is happy to shoulder the responsibilities involved. He looks forward to the Lord's day, for he delights in the privilege of ministering the Word of God to his people, and watching them grow in grace. His concern is for the men and women given into his care, not for himself or the prospects of personal gain.

This is good advice in a day when pastors' salaries are on the rise, comfortable parsonages are being provided, and fringe benefits are being increased. The "best pastorate" is not necessarily the one that pays the most, but the one God has called a man to accept. The rewards of the ministry are to be found in the lives of the people in the congregation, and in the Lord's blessing.

Serve Humbly and Purely

Peter's next exhortation contains a prohibition and a command. Church leaders are warned against becoming petty tyrants, but are instructed to be always worthy of imitation. Peter writes, "Neither as being lords over God's heritage, but being examples to the flock" (1 Peter 5:3). The tendency to be dictatorial is a common failing among church officials. Some men just can't handle authority without becoming autocratic. This may stem from pride or feelings of insecurity; but whatever the reason, it must be renounced.

Surprisingly, people are more inclined to become tyrannical when given a position of leadership over individuals they know. Almost anybody who works in a large factory or office, or who has served in the armed forces, will agree with this observation. Someone who has come up through the ranks tends to become proud and finds pleasure in giving orders. Since the officers in the early churches apparently were appointed from among the membership, this perhaps was a problem at that time. Paul declared that an elder should not be "a novice, lest being lifted up with pride he fall into the condemnation of the devil" (1 Tim. 3:6).

The positive side of Peter's exhortation is expressed in the words, "but being examples to the flock." The pastor leads by his godly life more than by the authority of his office. A shepherd *leads* sheep; he doesn't *drive* them.

Bossy, selfish, carnal, or immoral Christian leaders bring irreparable harm to the cause of Christ. Children in a church naturally look upon ministers with respect, for they expect them to be men of God. New believers, saved but still struggling with certain besetting sins, could well become disillusioned and completely discouraged if they were to see major flaws in the lives of people who have been Christians for many years. Every elder must lead, not by coercion or by pulling rank, but by the example of a life that is above reproach.

Responsibilities of the Younger

Peter now turns his attention to those whom he terms the "younger." We said earlier that the "elders" were men who held the office of bishop or pastor, and that the term may also have included other mature believers who held lesser positions of leadership. In speaking to the "younger," however, the apostle has in mind Christians of less maturity, either in spiritual development or in actual age. He says, "In like manner, ye younger, submit yourselves unto the elder. Yea, all of you be subject one to another, and be clothed with humility; for God resisteth the proud, and giveth grace to the humble" (1 Peter 5:5). Peter here sets forth two requirements for those who are younger in years or spiritual maturity: they are to be *submissive* and *humble* as they fulfill their roles in the church.

A Submissive Spirit

First, the younger are to acknowledge the God-given authority of the elders and submit to them. No organization can run efficiently unless this principle is followed. Until recently, a rebuke from church leaders was taken very seriously, at least in some fellowships. If a member fell into sin and did not repent, he was lovingly admonished, then solemnly warned, and finally, if he continued to be unrepentant, removed from the membership. When this announcement was made, a hush fell over the congregation and tears filled some eyes. But a breakdown in the matter of respect for authority has almost destroyed the effectiveness of disciplinary action in many churches today.

Something ought to be done about this situation, and it has to begin in each local congregation. Everyone who holds a position of leadership must consider it as a solemn trust, and church members must be taught to look upon their leaders as having been chosen by God. The writer of Hebrews issued a solemn command when he said, "Obey them that have the rule over you, and submit yourselves; for they watch for your souls, as they that must give account, that they may do it with joy, and not with grief; for that is unprofitable for you" (Heb. 13:17).

Perhaps the best place to begin cultivating an attitude of submission is in the home. By speaking respectfully of elders and deacons, the parents can set a good example for their children. This becomes a solid basis for building into the church once again that obedience to authority so essential to the spiritual health and happiness of its members.

Humility

The second admonition of the Apostle Peter is that believers be "clothed with humility." Peter was familiar with Satan's tactics. He knew that one of the enemy's major stratagems for destroying the effectiveness of a servant of Christ is to make him proud. We're especially susceptible to this form of attack if our service requires long hours with little pay, or brings us into contact with large numbers of people or with influential community leaders.

The best defense against pride is to remind ourselves continually of our weakness, our frailty, and our complete dependence upon God. We're to give Him the glory and praise in everything. As we do, we'll experience the promise first recorded in the Book of Proverbs and quoted here by Peter, "[God] giveth grace to the humble."

Reward For Obedience

The apostle's admonitions to "elders" and the "younger" were coupled with a promise of reward. He says first to the elders, "And when the Chief Shepherd shall appear, ye shall receive a crown of glory that fadeth not away" (1 Peter 5:4). Then, in relation to all believers, he declares, "Humble yourselves, therefore, under the mighty hand of God, *that He may exalt you in due time*" (1 Peter 5:6).

Every faithful child of God can look forward to a

day when the Lord will bestow great honor upon him. These rewards will be given "when the Chief Shepherd shall appear." Our Saviour is now invisible to our physical eyes, but when He returns, we will see Him face to face.

The prospect of Christ's second coming must have been especially precious to all of the apostles. They had lived with Jesus for over three years. They had talked with Him after His resurrection. They had seen Him ascend to heaven. Now, for 30 years or more they had not looked at Him or known His physical presence at their side. Oh yes, they knew where He was, and they sensed the reality of His *spiritual* presence, but they missed Him. How they longed for the day when they would look into His face again, and be with Him forever!

Peter, Paul, and John all wrote of the prospect of seeing Christ. As the beloved disciple put it, "Beloved, now are we the children of God, and it doth not yet appear what we shall be, but we know that, when He shall appear, we shall be like Him; for we shall see Him as He is" (1 John 3:2). The Lord Jesus, who as the "Good Shepherd" gave His life for us, and as the "Great Shepherd" is in heaven as our intercessor, will come again as the "Chief Shepherd" to take us to heaven.

In addition to seeing the Saviour and being with Him in heaven, we are promised "a crown of glory that fadeth not away" (v. 4). The Greek word translated "crown" can refer either to the quickly fading wreaths made of flowers and leaves, such as were won by athletes, or to the permanent golden crowns described by John in Revelation (see Rev. 4:10). Peter makes certain we know that he is referring to these everlasting crowns, for he declares that "our crown of glory" will be one "that fadeth not away."

In saying "fadeth not away," he uses a Greek term from which the *ameranth,* a flower that didn't wilt quickly when cut, derived its name. In Greek literature this plant with its unfading blossoms came to symbolize anything that remained beautiful forever. It is therefore a fitting image for the glory that awaits us.

The Bible contains many promises of rewards for the faithful—speaking often of crowns and of receiving glory. Just what does all this mean? Surely, more is implied than that we will walk around in heaven with heavy crowns on our heads. Then, too, the thought of "glory" must include more than being exalted above others or emitting light like an incandescent bulb. Since most people have a foggy notion of what the Bible means by "crowns," or "receiving glory," or "being glorified," it is well for us to do some serious thinking about rewards.

The promises of being commended and receiving different degrees of honor are not appeals to pride or a competitive spirit. God's approval and praise are the only rewards held before us. When we reach heaven, we will realize more than ever that salvation is by the Lord's grace alone. We will stand in amazement at the very fact that we are counted among the redeemed. To hear God say, "Well done!" or, "Enter thou into the joy of thy Lord!" will be the most thrilling yet humbling experience we've ever known.

This will be a humbling experience because on that day we will be vividly aware of two aspects of our relationship to God. First, we are creatures, made by Him and sustained by Him to do His will and bring glory to His name. We will be overwhelmed with joy and gratitude when we hear Him say that we fulfilled His purpose for our lives.

Second, we will be keenly conscious of our relationship as His children. Even as a youngster beams with delight when praised by his father or mother, upon whom he looks with great admiration, so we will be thrilled beyond words when our loving heavenly Father tells us He is pleased with us. We will be so filled with delight that there will be no room for pride. What a day that will be!

Christian friend, you may be a nobody in the eyes of your fellowmen, and sometimes even feel that way about yourself. In fact, you may have a dreadful inferiority complex, shrinking from public attention or from meeting "important" people. You may stay home from fellowship gatherings in your church, feeling that you are not wanted by the more affluent or talented people. But you can rejoice that God is someday going to give you personal recognition, public acknowledgment as His child, and a welcome into heaven. You are not an outsider. You are a member of God's family. You are the object of His special love and concern, a son or daughter in whom He delights. He has planned a special welcome for you on that day when you meet Him face to face. Yes, this glorious truth is humbling, but it should also give you a great sense of value and self-worth.

There is still another aspect of our coming glory. Very likely we will possess some kind of brilliance, perhaps similar to that which shone from Moses' face when he came down from Mount Sinai after receiving the Ten Commandments. It was seen in Jesus, too, on the Mount of Transfiguration.

Daniel spoke of this glory when he wrote, "And many of those who sleep in the dust of the earth shall awake, some to everlasting life, and some to shame and everlasting contempt. And they that be wise shall shine like the brightness of the firmament; and they that turn many to righteousness, as the stars forever and ever" (Dan. 12:2-3). Certainly this doesn't just mean that we will be like walking lights, each shining a little dimmer or brighter than the other. As the redeemed, we will be in perfect harmony with the infinite purity of heaven, where nothing sinful can enter.

Conclusion

Let me summarize by asking you this direct question: "Do you want a happy church?" If you do, the way to achieve it is not through being negative or hypercritical. You must be willing to do your part by taking positive action, and Peter has given the blueprint.

Speaking first to elders, he emphasized the importance of ministering faithfully to the flock. I recently heard of a pastor who was complaining bitterly about his last three churches. He had left them in turmoil, and in each case he blamed the people. I had a hard time believing it was as one-sided as he made it out to be.

If such a pastor were to seek my counsel, I would advise him to evaluate his ministry honestly in the light of 1 Peter 5:1-3. He should ask himself these questions: Am I serving willingly? Am I really happy in my role as shepherd of the flock? Or have I let personal gain become more important to me than my people's spiritual welfare? Am I insistent upon getting my own way? This pastor might see himself as being partly to blame, if he would measure his ministry by these guidelines.

If you are by your own opinion "just an average church member," don't underestimate the role you can fill to promote harmony and happiness in your congregation. By obeying Peter's exhortation to be submissive, and by earnestly seeking to be humble, you can "brighten the corner where you are." Even the most obstreperous and ornery church member won't be able to pick a fight with you if you wrap yourself in the garment of humility. In fact, he is likely to become ashamed of his wrong attitudes and start behaving more like a Christian. It's surprising how much influence can be exerted by a few persons who are truly Christlike. They can produce an atmosphere which makes the fellowship of the saints here on earth a foretaste of heaven. Yes, you *can* have a *happy church!*

12

Now Until Then

(1 Peter 5:8-14)

If you had been a member of one of the churches in
Asia Minor, I'm sure you would have been thrilled
and encouraged as you heard Peter's letter being
read by your pastor. Thinking back over its con-
tents, you'd likely say, "That's quite an epistle!" And
you'd be right.

Let's review for a moment what Peter said. He
had begun by clarifying our identity as elect sojourners, had emphasized our security in Christ,
and had said much about the kind of persons God
expects us to be. He had soared to the heights, referring to our "joy unspeakable and full of glory."
He had given specific teaching on many of the basic
truths of the Christian faith, and made Christ's
person and ministry come alive to us. And, he had
included practical suggestions on how to live successfully in the home, the church, and the community.

The letter had its somber passages as well. Peter
had descended into the valleys of Christian experience, speaking of the hardships, difficulties, and

145

persecution often encountered by faithful believers in Christ. In so doing, he repeatedly had pointed us to the Lord Jesus as our example in suffering. He encouraged us to live in confidence and hope, to be steadfast in the faith, and to commit our souls to God. And, time after time, he lifted our eyes from this present life to the eternity of happiness and glory that awaits us in heaven.

But now Peter is ready to draw his letter to a close. He's concerned about the spiritual welfare of these believers, for he knows they will soon be facing turbulent times and severe trials. He therefore concludes his epistle with three practical parting words—advice we all are to follow if we wish to retain our Christian integrity and fulfill our mission here on earth. As recorded in 1 Peter 5:8-14, we must (1) be vigilant, (2) assess the situation correctly, and (3) keep before us the promises of God.

Maintain a Ceaseless Vigil

The first word of advice is for believers in Christ to be levelheaded and on the alert. Peter says, "Be sober, be vigilant" (1 Peter 5:8). In this double command, two Greek words leap out in abrupt staccato. The first, translated "be sober," tells us to maintain serious, disciplined self-control at all times. We're not to let emotional extremes—fear, panic, anger—get the best of us. We're to keep a clear mind and firm grip on ourselves, lest we fall easy prey to the enemy of our souls and bring dishonor to the name of Christ. The second, "be vigilant," means we are to keep on the alert and be watchful at all times. Just as a city under threat of attack maintains a 24-hour lookout for the enemy, so we must be always on guard. We're not ever to let down, not even for a second!

Peter very likely was writing these words with deep emotion. He may have been thinking of an experience in his own life, an event recorded for us in the Gospels. The Lord Jesus, you will recall, had asked Peter, James, and John to "watch and pray" when He entered the Garden of Gethsemane. They fell asleep, however, and as a consequence were spiritually unprepared for the events of the next few hours.

Just a short time later, a band of soldiers came to arrest Jesus. Peter foolishly took out his sword and cut off a man's ear. Within minutes all the disciples had fled, including Peter. Later that night he shamefully denied his Lord three times.

Oh yes, the Saviour forgave him and restored him to fellowship, but you can be sure it hurt Peter deeply whenever he remembered what he had done that night. If only he had been watching and praying instead of sleeping! If only he had controlled his emotions instead of frantically trying to fight with the sword! As Peter reflected upon that bitter experience, he knew the value of maintaining self-control and a constant vigil, and warned all who would read his epistle to keep up their guard.

The Bible itself contains many illustrations confirming the wisdom of the exhortation, "Be sober, be vigilant." It was while Samson lay asleep on the lap of Delilah that his locks were cut off, with the result that he lost his great strength and was captured by the enemy. It was while David was relaxing at his palace that he allowed his passions to get the better of him. He took a second lustful look, and as a result he fell into a deep abyss of sin, committing both adultery and murder. How appropriate Peter's admonition, "Be sober, be watchful!" Self-control and continual alertness are absolute necessities for Christians who live as aliens in a hostile environment.

Know the True Situation

The apostle's second parting word gives us the reason for alertness and steadfastness. We have a deadly enemy and should be aware of his strategy. We read, "Be sober, be vigilant, because your adversary, the devil, like a roaring lion walketh about, seeking whom he may devour; whom resist steadfast in the faith, knowing that the same afflictions are accomplished in your brethren that are in the world" (1 Peter 5:8-9). Peter here identifies the enemy of our souls, describes his activity, and tells us to oppose him.

This evil foe is called "your adversary, the devil," and is none other than Satan. A powerful angelic being who once had a position of great glory and honor in heaven, Satan fell into sin and consequently was banished from God's presence. These events are described in Isaiah 14 and Ezekiel 28. In calling him "your adversary," Peter uses the Greek word *antidikos,* which denotes an opponent in a lawsuit. In a more general sense, it refers to anyone who is against us. This is also the meaning of the proper name "Satan" which designates him as our "adversary." The word "devil" is a transliteration of *diabolos,* which literally means "one who throws over" or "one who throws across." The word is used to denote an accuser or slanderer.

Taken together, these names for Satan portray him as a bitter enemy determined to destroy us, using slander or accusation as his primary weapons. His malicious and destructive purposes are indicated by Peter's description that he "like a roaring lion walketh about, seeking whom he may devour."

But sometimes he puts on a deceptively appealing front, for Paul tells us, "Satan himself is transformed into an angel of light" (2 Cor. 11:14). His goal is always the same however—to destroy mankind.

A vast majority of people in our 20th-century world do not see the enemy of our souls as the Bible presents him. Many refuse to believe he exists, thinking of him as a mythological representation of impishness or mischief. Others worship him as some sort of god of the sensuous, and adopt a life of unrestrained wickedness. They too are deceived, for Satan is real, he is evil, and his aim is their destruction.

Jesus described Satan's evil character and purpose when He said to the Pharisees, "Ye are of your father the devil, and the lusts of your father ye will do. He was a *murderer* from the beginning, and abode not in the truth, because there is no truth in him. When he speaketh a lie, he speaketh of his own; for *he is a liar,* and the father of it" (John 8:44). The wise Christian never underestimates this fierce enemy!

Believers must face up to their inability to overcome Satan without the help of God. After all, we are but weak and frail creatures living as aliens in a topsy-turvy world, while he is a powerful spiritual being who heads up a great army of fallen angels. If we were to depend upon our strength only, we certainly could never defeat him. A 1,000-pound tiger and a 150-pound man would be far more evenly matched than any one of us against Satan.

With divine help, however, we *can* overcome Satan, and Peter suggests how. He says, "Whom resist steadfast in the faith." The Greek word translated "resist" means to "withstand," and is a term of defense, not of attack. Having declared ourselves to be God's children and our determination to do His will, we're to stand our ground. Furthermore, we are to withstand "steadfast in the faith." This means we must depend wholly upon the Lord. When we do, we call His omnipotence into play on our side, and success is guaranteed.

James confirms this method of doing battle with Satan when he says, "Submit yourselves, therefore, to God. Resist the devil, and he will flee from you" (James 4:7).

Peter comforts believers by telling them that "the same afflictions are accomplished in your brethren that are in the world" (1 Peter 5:9). Sometimes when we're under heavy attack by the enemy, we feel isolated. It seems that we're the only ones being called upon to undergo what we're facing. These early believers were reminded, therefore, not to think of themselves as special targets of Satan's wrath or as facing a unique situation for which God had no remedy. The Lord, for reasons we cannot fully understand, sometimes permits the enemy to bring terrific pressure to bear upon followers of Jesus. But whenever Christians go through such an experience, it is comforting to realize that thousands of fellow believers have experienced the same kind of trouble, and in time have come through triumphantly.

In summary, every child of God must accept the biblical teachings about Satan and follow its directions for avoiding his snares. If he puts these truths into practice, he will be victorious, for the Apostle John assures us, "Greater is He [the Holy Spirit] that is in you, than he [Satan] that is in the world" (1 John 4:4). When you faithfully follow the teaching of the Bible, and call upon the help of God, the "roaring lion" will slink away in defeat.

Three Truths to Keep in Mind

Having exhorted us to be spiritually alert and to
resist the attacks of the enemy, Peter presents three
basic truths to help us live in victory. He first reminds us of God's grace, then assures us that our
suffering is for "awhile," and finally tells us that
the Lord uses it for our own good. He writes, "But
the God of all grace, who hath called us unto His
eternal glory by Christ Jesus, after ye have suffered
awhile, make you perfect, establish, strengthen,
settle you" (1 Peter 5:10).

As God's children living in a hostile world, we're
bound to face times when we're lonely and dis-
heartened. We may even be tempted to give up. But
the greatest antidote for discouragement is a fresh
reminder that we serve "the God of *all grace*." What
a magnificent expression! Grace is the Lord's favor
upon us as undeserving sinners. It reaches into
every aspect of our lives. In the opening words of
1 Peter we were told it was in *grace* that God chose
us to salvation. It was through *grace* that He saved
us by faith in His Son. He forgives our sins daily
by *grace* as we confess them. Through *grace* we
can stand true in hardship and persecution. By
the power of His *grace* we are sustained in the hour
of death.

A little girl was watching her mother pour liquid
gelatin into several dessert molds of various shapes
and sizes. She was amazed that each would come
out different, conformed to the shape of the mold.
She exclaimed in wonder, "Oh, Mother! It fits them
all!" Just so with "the manifold grace of God"
(1 Peter 4:10). Whatever the demands of a varied
and complex life, God's grace "fits them all." And
this brings confidence and encouragement to every
believer determined to serve the Lord.

The second comforting truth to remember is that our suffering is temporary. He says, "After ye have suffered awhile." We are called and destined to a glory that is eternal, and the suffering confronting us is, by comparison, only of brief duration. The Apostle Paul speaks of "our light affliction, which is but for a moment" (2 Cor. 4:17).

Sometimes the hours and days seem to go by very slowly. A person on a bed of illness and pain may long for evening, which seems as if it will never come; but then through the hours of the night he will yearn for the breaking of dawn. But the few years we spend down here are almost nothing when compared to the endless ages of bliss that await us. When we reach heaven, and view life on earth from the vantage point of eternity, we'll know how brief the time of suffering has really been. The words of this little poem by an unknown author express it well:

A little while, and we shall be
  Where sin can never dwell;
A little while, and we shall live
  Where songs of triumph swell.
A little while, and we shall hear
  Our Saviour's whisper, "Come!"
And we shall ever dwell with Him
  In our eternal Home.
A little while, and we shall see
  Our Saviour face to face,
And we shall sing, through endless days,
  The wonders of His grace.

The third truth called to the attention of believers is that the afflictions suffered here are permitted by the Lord for our eternal good. We may be hated by the world and attacked by the forces of Satan, but through it all God is preparing us for heaven.

Using four verbs, Peter shows how the fires of affliction will enrich us for all eternity. He says God will "make you perfect, establish, strengthen, settle you" (1 Peter 5:10).

1. *Make you perfect*—The Lord perfects His children through trial and testing. The verb means "to put in order" or "to complete" or "to put into proper condition." It is used to refer to the mending of nets (Mark 1:19), and in classical Greek it was the term used to designate the setting of a fracture, the repair of anything broken, or the supply of a missing part. As we go through fiery trials, therefore, we are made perfect, missing elements in our character are supplied, and faults are eliminated.

Barclay illustrates this truth as follows:

> It is said that Sir Edward Elgar once listened to a young girl singing one of the solos from one of his own works. She had a voice of exceptional purity and clarity and range, a voice like that of a boy soprano. She had an almost perfect technique which made light of the technical difficulties of the solo. When she had finished singing, Sir Edward said softly, "She will be really great when something happens to break her heart." (William Barclay, *The Letters of James and Peter:* Westminster Press, Philadelphia.)

2. *Establish you*—The Greek word translated "establish" means "to support," "to set up," or "to fix firmly." Suffering gives a yielded Christian that quality which makes his behavior and reactions predictable. Such a person isn't wild with excitement and joy one moment, only to fall apart emotionally the next. He develops a spiritual stability which enables him to stand true in every test. The Lord adapts the difficulty to our strength, and when we

trust Him day by day, He gives us grace to withstand the most grievous affliction without despair. Even as men use fire to temper steel, so the Lord uses the fiery trials of life to "establish" us.

3. *Strengthen you*—The third benefit that comes through suffering is that God uses it to "make us strong." The word rendered "strengthen" is not found any other place in the New Testament. Some scholars translate it "filled with might," and relate it to Paul's teaching where he speaks of our being "strengthened with might by His Spirit in the inner man" (Eph. 3:16). Through suffering we become strong-hearted and strong-willed, that we may resist the onslaughts of Satan and effectively serve the Lord.

4. *Settle you*—The final benefit Peter mentions is that God will "settle" us through affliction. The verb selected by Peter for use here means "to found" or "to lay the foundation." When persecution or hardship occur, we become keenly aware of the very foundation of our faith. Our adverse experiences give us a deeper appreciation for the great truths upon which our Christianity is grounded. We are thus weaned from self-confidence and from trust in external ceremonies or rituals.

Many Christians have testified that in the crucible of trial they saw more clearly than ever before the truth that their salvation is based totally on the work of the Lord Jesus. All incidentals fell away, and they were driven to the bedrock of their faith— the death, resurrection, ascension, and intercessory ministry of Christ.

In closing, let me emphasize again that God has not granted us immunity from affliction just because we are Christians. These times are bound to come, and they are not without purpose. They give us the opportunity for spiritual growth. They can be the means by which we develop into glowing witnesses for Christ, so that we become effective in leading others to Him. And, they result in everlasting riches for us in the glory that awaits.

This is the "good news for bad times" from Peter. God knows all about our trials. More than that, He permits them for our eternal benefit. We *can* be victorious in every circumstance as we call upon the help of God. We can overcome Satan and experience true joy and abiding peace.

We are not surprised, therefore, that Peter closes his epistle with the benediction, "Peace be with you all that are in Christ Jesus. Amen" (1 Peter 5:14). He was returning to the same thought he had expressed in his salutation, "Grace unto you, and peace, be multiplied" (1 Peter 1:2).

Peter knew from experience that God gives a blessed tranquillity and calmness of spirit to all who trust in Him. Some 35 years had passed since he had heard Jesus, on the night of His arrest in Gethsemane, tell His frightened and bewildered disciples, "Peace I leave with you, My peace I give unto you; not as the world giveth, give I unto you. Let not your heart be troubled, neither let it be afraid" (John 14:27). Peter had found that Jesus keeps His word! And this peace is still being experienced by God's children today.

An aged Christian man recently gave testimony to the peace of God from his hospital bed. Knowing life for him was drawing to a close, he told his pastor, "When I came to the Lord 58 years ago, He took away the burden of my sin and gave me peace. Since that day I've known poverty, grief, and suffering. My wife and three of my children have preceded me in death. But through it all, my Saviour never left me. Now, as I depart this earth, I have the same peace in my heart He gave me more than half a century ago."

Isn't that exactly like Peter's epistle? It begins with peace, in between are troubles, difficulties, and persecution, but it ends with peace. And that's the way it can be for you, as you appropriate the good news of this epistle to your life. Do it! And you will praise God with "joy unspeakable, and full of glory!"